Pearls:
Wisdom & Insight For The Life You Live Today
by Earl Bryant

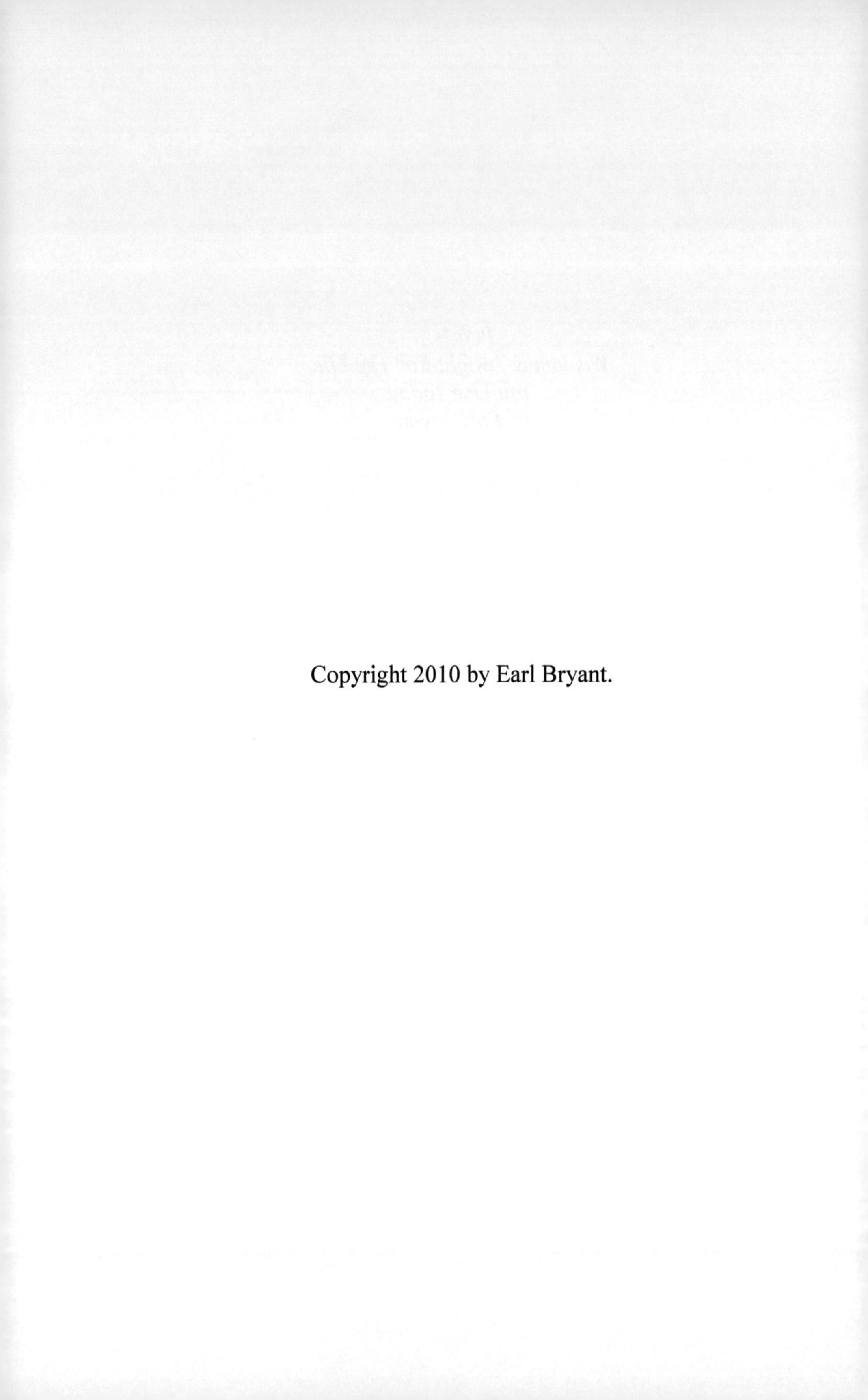

Acknowledgments

First and foremost, all the glory and honor and praise for this project go to the Most High God, the God of Abraham, Isaac, and Jacob. He is the reason I was able to complete this project, for it is in Him that I live and move and have my being. Without His guidance and direction I would not have the ability to write, nor would I possess the inspiration to do so. So I acknowledge Him first, and to Him above all, I give thanks.

To acknowledge all the people He has brought to my life to inspire and influence me would require volumes of books to recognize. There are several however that deserve particular recognition.

To the teachers of the Uniondale School District on Long Island, NY: California Avenue School, Lawrence Rd. Jr. High School, Uniondale High School, to Kingsborough Comm. College of the City University of NY, and to the University of Bridgeport, Connecticut: I say thank you for kindling within me a desire for learning which burns brightly to this day.

To the Wachovia CIC Toastmasters Club 7358, District 37 of Charlotte, NC, I say thank you for teaching me communication and leadership skills, and for reminding me that every polished speaker endures the brief period of "...dry mouth, sweaty palms, pounding heart, and the knocking knees," all of which are part of the path one travels before becoming a seasoned communicator.

To the Full Gospel Tabernacle of Massapequa, NY (also known as the Long Island Revival Center), to Victorious Life Church of Charleston, SC, and to Victory Christian Center of Charlotte, NC, led by such solid pastors and men of God as Eugene Profeta, Gene Harmon, and Robyn Gool , I thank you for the Word of God you bring forth without compromise, and for challenging me to grow in all areas of my life. You all have my gratitude and thanks for continuing to take such a strong stand in favor of the things of God.

To the people of WritersDigest.com, I say thanks for providing your passion and instruction in the craft of writing. I never before realized writing can be a rewarding profession until I learned of the great people involved with your organization. Thank you for all your guidance and direction.

To the people of Lulu.com, I say thank you for helping me with my first publishing endeavor. Thank you for removing all the mystery from the self-publishing process. You have inspired me to initiate future projects, and for that I am grateful.

To all the people who supported me throughout the entire process of putting this book together, you have my gratitude, today and always. You helped make this happen; there are no words that can describe my appreciation for you. Thank you all.

Dedication

To my family, my wife Tuesday, my son Earl III, and my daughter Kaitlyn: You are my motivation to excel, the reason I persist in every endeavor. I thank you for loving me, and allowing me to love you.

To my parents, Earl Sr. and Delores:
Thank you for showing me how to choose joy in the midst of any storm and any challenge. And for your example to me from childhood that one always brings their best when things seem to be at their worst. I love and appreciate you both more than words could express.

To my sisters, Tiffany, Karen, Tina and Pam:
You gave guidance and direction in four different ways, all unique, all distinct, all different, yet all important. Living under the same roof with you during our childhood was and adventure, a joy and a pleasure, and the pleasure was all mine. I am most privileged and blessed to have sisters like you. I could have chosen none better. I hope one day to be half as good a brother to you as you have been sisters to me.

To my grandparents, James Frederick Bryant Sr., Pauline Murphy Bryant, James "Bub" Brown, Sr., and Ruth Helen Johnson Brown:

Thank you for blazing a trail for your descendants to follow. Thank you also for showing that joy is a choice, and that while it may be a bit difficult to find a reason to smile at times, doing so is always worth the effort. Thank you for leading the way.

Introduction

Let me take a moment to thank you for deciding to read this book. As there are other things you could be doing with your valuable time, I'm so honored that you've invested some of your time viewing these pages.

Pearls are items that have long been associated with great value. It has been said that the most valuable commodity you can possess is wisdom. So consider this book to be a collection of wisdom that has been shared with me over the past many years, wisdom which I gladly pass along to you.

I wrote this book with one objective, and that was to provide motivation, inspiration, information, and education to help you navigate successfully through the "waters" of daily living. Should none of these apply, then I hope to give you something worthwhile to ponder as you continue your life's journey.

It is not my intent to lecture, or to "preach" at you. Please forgive me if I come across that way. I have no such intention. I just aim to encourage you and strengthen you for the challenges you face. And if we don't see eye to eye on what I've written, we can respectfully agree to disagree. I ask only that you allow me a chance to share my views, then after I do so, please feel free to draw your own conclusions. Fair enough?

With that being said, let me officially welcome you to Pearls, with the hope that you find the wisdom you need to help you meet the everyday problems you face.

Read and reap...

Be blessed...and enjoy!

EB

Table of Contents

1. Give Yourself Permission To Succeed

Do you remember when we were kids? As infants and babies, we pretty much got what we wanted, because our wants and needs were very basic and very simple. Eat. Sleep. Numbers 1 and 2. You get the idea. When we got a bit older we learned that a little more tact was in order. We had to ask for what we wanted, because we needed permission to do what we wanted. We couldn't just take what we felt like taking as kids, we had to get approval from Mom and Dad first. And so it went for most of our childhood.

Then we became adults. Notice I didn't say we all grew up. I just said we became adults. I made this distinction with good reason. You'll see why in a moment.

As adults we are expected to make decisions, to assume responsibility for our decisions, and to accept the consequences of decisions we make, for better or worse. This unfortunately is where many adults miss the boat. Many are still stuck in that childhood phase that says permission must be granted before making any significant moves.

But when you're an adult it's a double whammy. Why? Because adults often hold back in two ways. On one hand, we hold ourselves back from things we want to do by hiding behind so called responsibilities (Something that sounds like, "I'd like to, but I can't, I have to..." comes to mind. Ring a bell?)

On the other hand, we hold fast to rules once imposed for our own good in childhood, rules which no longer apply. We look for someone to give us permission to do things we really want to do, and know we are fully capable of doing. Not just because we want permission granted to do what's in our hearts, but I believe also because we want someone else to take the blame, the fall, the "heat," the responsibility, if we pursue our dreams, our goals, and things fall apart. Just that attitude itself indicates a major lack of maturity, personal responsibility, and accountability.

We used to raise children in this nation to be trustworthy, dependable adults, knowing they were mature enough to handle the consequences of their actions, for better or worse. Nowadays, we have too many people who want to point fingers at everyone around in an effort to take as much of the attention off of themselves as they possibly can. As a result we lose our courage, we lose our nerve, we lose our sense of initiative, and we waste valuable opportunities for growth. Worst of all we lose in the long run the most precious commodity we could ever hope to gain:

RESPECT

The respect of others, sure. That's a given, but the worst kind of respect we can lose is self-respect. Our dignity. Our sense of worth and value. So much so that not only can we not look others in the eye, but we also cannot look ourselves in the mirror. And yet with all that we stand to lose, the solution is so very simple as to boggle the mind. Before you can give yourself that respect, before you can earn the respect of others, you need something far greater. Something that will untie your hands, break the chains, free you from the bondage that holds you back. That something you need is simply called PERMISSION. And that permission can be granted to you by only one person. The same person holding the keys that keep you in chains, keep you in bondage, and hold you down.

It's not your mama.
It's not your daddy.
It's not family, friends, co workers, in-laws (or outlaws).
It's not even your enemies.

IT'S YOU. YES, YOU!!!

And how do you release yourself, set yourself free to pursue your dreams?

You let go of your past failures, your past grudges, your past flaws, your past hurts, your past anger, bitterness, resentment, insecurities, envies, jealousies, comparisons, anxieties, doubts, even your past fears.

Let go of it. ALL of it. By forgiving. Forgiving yourself.

When most people speak of forgiveness, rarely do they consider extending forgiveness to themselves. It's the furthest thing from their minds. But take a look at this scripture, and I'll show you what most people overlook:

"And whenever you stand praying, if you have anything against anyone, forgive him and let it drop (leave it, let it go), in order that your Father Who is in heaven may also forgive you your [own] failings and shortcomings and let them drop. But if you do not forgive, neither will your Father in heaven forgive your failings and shortcomings."- Mark 11:25-26

In this passage what people don't realize is that "anyone" includes themselves. They also don't comprehend that forgiveness is not earned, it is granted. It is extended. Many times we say we're mad at someone else and don't see that we are really mad at ourselves. We feel we're between a rock and a hard place because we want to hurt the person responsible for hurting us, and often that very person is us. We get frustrated because we can't "get back" at ourselves. We can't get even with ourselves. So we stew in and resentment unless we let go of the judgment, condemnation and grudges we use to keep ourselves in bondage.

Forgiving is like releasing someone from prison, only to learn the one behind bars was you.

If you're wondering why it seems that others can get ahead while you cannot, take a good look at your heart. If you have a heart full of grudges, bitterness, resentment, hatred, or unforgiveness against yourself, then the answer is clear. Here's what you need to do:

Release yourself from the following:
- a hard heart
- bitterness
- resentment
- grudges
- judgment
- condemnation
- guilt
- hopelessness
- despair
- depression
- despondency

And most of all, release yourself from your past. ALL of it. You cannot go back to the past and change it. But you can move forward from where you are right now.

"Forgiveness cannot change the past, but it does enlarge the future." - William Arthur Ward

But until you forgive, there is no future to move toward because you're clinging to memories that continue to hold you back.

So forgive yourself. Release yourself from your past. Let it go. Then and only then will you be able to give yourself permission to succeed.

Read it and reap...

Be blessed...

And we'll talk again...

2. Stir Up Your Gift

When most people think of gifts, what comes to mind are items received during special occasions: birthdays, anniversaries, Christmas, Hanukah, or any other occasion where gift giving is deemed appropriate. The main premise of gifts in this instance concerns those that are received.

But I want to talk to you about gifts in a different sense. You already possess these gifts, but unlike the conventional gifts we earlier spoke of, these do not belong to you alone. They are to be shared. Your talents. Your abilities. Your interests. Your passion. Yes, I said your passion, that which burns inside you. That passion you have is an urgency, an all consuming desire you need to express. And the reason you have that yearning to express your unique skills is because there are people in the world, most of whom you do not yet know, that require you to share your gift. Or your gifts; you could have more than one that you need to share. They need to be unleashed because people need the blessing your gift has to offer. You may not see the value of your unique abilities. But others do. They know the world will not be as good or as magnificent as it could be, unless you express the beauty of the gift within you.

I can hear your protests now, so let's get them out of the way:

But I don't have a gift or any special ability...
(Yes, you do)

But I don't have any talent...(Yes you have)

But I'm not capable of expressing myself...(Yes you are)

But I don't measure up to those who are more established, more gifted, more talented, more special, more unique, etc...
(Says who? And even if it's true that you don't, SO WHAT?)

Time for a reality check here. Other people are not your standard, your benchmark, your measuring stick, or your point of reference. Besides, it's not all that smart to compare yourself to another man or woman who is just as imperfect as you are:

"Let such a person consider this, that what we are in word by letters when we are absent, such we will also be in deed when we are present. For we dare not class ourselves or compare ourselves with those who commend themselves. But they, measuring themselves by themselves, and comparing themselves among themselves, are not wise." - II Corinthians 10:11,12

"Too many people overvalue what they are not and undervalue what they are."
- Malcolm Forbes

Here's something else you should know: if the people in your circle do not appreciate the unique skills you have, understand that they are not the intended recipients of your gifts. Most likely the people who you will bless the most with your talents are people you don't know, and who don't know you...YET. So stir up your gift! There are people that need the blessings you can bestow upon them!

"That is why I would remind you to stir up (rekindle the embers of, fan the flame of, and keep burning) the [gracious] gift of God, [the inner fire] that is in you..." - II Timothy 1:6

Rekindle the dormant embers of your gifts. Fan the flames of your talents, keep them burning. Forge ahead in pursuit of those achievements you have long desired to attain. And do it quickly, for there are people in this world who not only long for the blessing you have in store for them, but they need what you have to offer so desperately.

And remember, as you put your talents on display for all to see and enjoy, not only will their lives forever be changed, but so will yours, for as you allow your gifts to be demonstrated, and as the natural fragrance of your personality flows from within you to every life you touch, you will begin to see, experience, and enjoy a fresh look at life through a brand new set of eyes. So whatever you must do to make it happen, do it quickly. Time is of the essence, and valuable lives hang in the balance. Fan the flames, stir up your gifts, and make each encounter in your day a special occasion.

Read it and reap...

Be blessed everybody...

And we'll talk again...

3. Do What You're Afraid Of

Do you know that there's a correlation between what you want to do and what you fear doing? It is simply this: what you are afraid of is a major barrier to your success. What you fear is also a major component to your success, for your victory lies in the ability to overcome fear and doubt. As fear is coupled with doubt, attaining that goal may seem impossible, if not insurmountable. The big problem with so many of us is that we work so hard to build up images of difficulty, resistance, and opposition in our own minds, the "mountain" appears to be a summit so tough to conquer, we become too intimidated to even approach it.

We need to realize is that the very first obstacle we must tackle is not outside of ourselves, but within us. We must get past the barrier that we have erected with our own minds, and our own vision (or lack thereof). If we took half the energy we used to make excuses, and instead made decisions and commitments, then took action toward those decisions and commitments with firm resolve, we'd be amazed and astonished at the results we would see.

It doesn't matter what the challenge is. It could be skydiving, or public speaking, it could be playing a musical instrument, or swimming, sailing, flying a plane, writing a book, finishing school, getting licensed, certified, whatever. You may be unsure that you'll ever master your challenges, but if you don't confront your challenges, it is absolutely guaranteed you will not overcome them.

"You miss 100% of the shots you don't take." - Wayne Gretzky

You may be surprised to learn the victory you desire can be found in the midst of the biggest challenge you face. When you run toward your problem, when you run to the battle, much like the young warrior David ran toward the giant named Goliath, you find out your problem is not nearly as big as you feared. You will see your problem shrink in proportion to the size and magnitude of the action you take in mastering your challenge.

And consider this, too: your challenge is not powerful enough to take you out. It is not designed to destroy you, but rather to develop you. To strengthen you. To build you.

Do you know that when you exercise, whether it's your body or your mind, it is the very process of engaging the challenge that causes your strength to grow, your confidence to build, your ability to increase. In bodybuilding especially, the term that is used to describe the training process of lifting weights to build muscle definition and mass is known as "resistance." Your encounter with this resistance makes your strength grow, makes your ability grow, makes your confidence increase. It is only when a vessel experiences the challenges, the adversities that the open sea affords, that such a ship can known as "seaworthy". The process of attaining such worthiness among mankind is no different:

"A ship in a harbor is safe. But that's not what ships were made for." - Pastor Robyn Gool

If you are someone who feels fear about facing your challenge, your mountain, then let me encourage you. Just because you feel fear, just because you are scared of your challenge, your problem, does not mean you cannot in some way overcome it and master it. That fear simply means you do not yet know you can. It shouldn't prevent you from taking the needed steps to find out.

If you feel afraid while taking on your obstacle, then do it afraid until you achieve your goal, and you may find out that somewhere along the way you stopped being afraid.

"You'll never conquer what you're not willing to confront." - Pastor Andre Landers

You can believe for your victory before you act, but you receive the victory as you act. Victory requires motion. Don't fall into the trap known as "paralysis by analysis." You many be scared to act because you think you'll fail. Let me tell you something: the only time you know for sure that you will fail is if you don't try, if you don't even bother to make an effort. And if you do try and things don't work out, so what? That setback does not mean you failed. It just means you haven't succeeded yet. You see, failure is never fatal, and failure is never final. While completing work on one of his many inventions, a great American innovator once made this statement:

"I have not failed. I've just found 10,000 ways that won't work." - Thomas Alva Edison (1847-1931)

It is that same approach, that same position, that same attitude, that you must carry if you are to ultimately achieve the success you seek, desire, the success you deserve. Don't be discouraged by setbacks, and don't give in to despair. In every life there are seasons, and adversity, setbacks, and disappointments can only last for a season. Van Crouch often says that problems have "...a limited life span." Problems are like storms, which in a small way are like seasons. No matter how things seem, no matter how tough things may get, these difficult times are not designed to last. They don't have the power to sustain themselves. But you do.

You have an ability that storms do not have. You have the ability to regroup, rebuild, to re-gather your strength. Once a storm has blown through, all it can do is weaken and dissipate. Just knowing that should give you power to face and master your challenges, overcome your adversities. You can outwit, outmaneuver and outlast any problem that comes against you.

Know most of all that tough times cannot last, but tough people can. And tough people do. And if you are reading this message, I'm talking about you.

You are here on earth for a season, and for a reason.

You were born on purpose, for a purpose.

You have no time to lose.

You are only here to win.

So whatever it is you are afraid of, rise to the occasion, rise to meet your challenge.
For it is in the midst of your fear that you will find your strength, your courage, and best of all, your victory.

Read it and reap...

Be blessed....

And we'll talk again...

4. Stop Beating Yourself Up

I get very concerned about people I know who act as their own worst enemy. They seem to take great pleasure in finding fault with themselves, picking apart their lives with the morbid curiosity used to dissect a frog, dredging up wounds, shortcomings, and insecurities.

Now don't misunderstand, I'm not talking about those who simply acknowledge their imperfections. That's something we all have in common, and such an admission can relieve stress at times. It can even be therapeutic. I'm referring to those people who seem to make a career of accentuating the negative, overplaying and blowing out of proportion those moments of which they are not proud.

What they fail to realize is that everybody has such moments, everybody suffers embarrassment about something at some time their lives. That's part of the charm of being human. What happens to some, however, is that they dwell on these not so great moments so often, they seem to create a continuous long running miniseries, soap opera, and reality show of the everyday details which make up their existence. I suppose you could say their perception fuels their perspective.

What too often happens is that we take these difficult moments, these setbacks, to heart and mistakenly believe these fleeting incidents define our identity. As in, "I failed, so I must be a failure." Discouragement can set in, and depression can take hold of us, keeping us captive if we don't pay attention to what's happening and take steps to limit the potential damage, which could prevent us from falling into such a trap.

What we don't often see, don't understand, and fail to recognize, is that we all enter the earth in the same fashion. We are not frightfully made, we are wonderfully made. We all have potential for greatness, achievement and accomplishment deposited within us. The reason this seems to be a false notion is because some of us have been encouraged to develop our potential, while others have been mocked, even ridiculed for doing so.

If you've ever seen the movie "Twiins," with Arnold Schwarzenegger and Danny DeVito, you may understand what I mean. Arnold & Danny played fraternal twins, developed in a laboratory by doctors to be an ideal specimen, an optimally functioning human being. Arnold's character Julius was, that is. Danny's character, Vincent, was an unintended sidekick, an "oops," if you will. After having met the pair in adulthood, one of the doctors gave a classic example of how people are treated and mistreated, sometimes in lockstep with one another. While explaining the process by which they were brought into the world, the doctor explained that everything that was good, upright, and upstanding went into developing Julius, and that (doctor's words, not mine) "all the crap" went into Vincent.

I realize that was just a movie, but how would you like to be referred to in such fashion? That would be pretty rough, I imagine. As bad as that sounds, how much worse must it be when the person who believes, and says, that you are comprised of "all the crap," is none other than you? It's like a comic strip from days gone by, named "Pogo," where the main character so eloquently describes a situation of his own making: "We have met the enemy, an' he is us..." Too many people are their own worst enemy. They bludgeon themselves mercilessly, and they do it non-stop.

There are more than enough people who are all too willing to do whatever it takes to bring you down and keep you down. Why make it easier for them to do so by volunteering for that duty? Why would you praise and honor the Creator, yet denounce, and denigrate His prize creation? It makes not one bit of sense. You have no trouble accepting, acknowledging, and appreciating others. You need to be willing to do the same thing for yourself.

Understand this: you have value. You have something worthwhile to contribute during your days on the earth. Don't waste your precious time denigrating and dissipating your potential. Use that valuable share of riches that has been deposited within you and leave the world a better place than you found it.

And while you're traveling your life's journey, take the advice I once received from a sign I read upon entering a county park on Long Island:

Take nothing but pictures
Leave nothing but footprints

Take your place,
Make your mark, and:

STOP BEATING YOURSELF UP!

Read it and reap...

Be blessed everyone...

And we'll talk again....

5. Is Something Holding You Back?

Are there things in your life that you've always wanted to accomplish? Goals you set, but for some reason you put them on the back burner? Have your "I want to be ... when I grow up" desires turned into "I wish I had done ... when I had the chance" regrets? If you find yourself saying or thinking along these lines, then maybe something (or someone) is holding you back, mentally barring you from stepping out and taking a risk to do what you've always wanted to do.

You may have had a legitimate reason when you were younger not to pursue those goals, those objectives. Maybe back then it was because you had elders, parents, guardians, who looked out for you and tried to do their best to protect you. Maybe they had your best interests at heart when they tried to guide you in another direction. That would seem a sensible course of action during your childhood, for they didn't want you to get hurt.

But what about now? You may be an adult. By adult I don't necessarily mean you've just become "legal", as in 21 years of age, or even just a bit older, say 25 or 27 years of age. You may be in your 30s. Or your 40s. You could even be in your 50s or older, with the chance to do things you wanted to do when you were younger, yet you still won't take the plunge. Why? Could it be because you're still holding on to memories of the past, where those people who "knew what was best for you" still hold sway in your current existence? Or could it be that as a child you obeyed without question whatever your elders told you to do, or not to do, and you never got past living up to that expectation, even if those elders are no longer around? Let's say you've gotten past that hurdle somehow, but you still feel restricted. Maybe you're afraid to step out, to put yourself "out there," because you're paralyzed with fear about "what people may think" about you.

If any of what you've just read describes you, don't feel ashamed or embarrassed. What you're feeling is actually quite normal, and anxieties take place, not because of what you know, but because of what you do not know. For instance, when you fear what people may think, it is simply because you do not know what they think, and you're afraid of what would happen if you ever found out.

If that is the case, it may help you if I answer that question for you. Here's what people think:

THEY THINK WHATEVER THEY PLEASE, WHENEVER THEY PLEASE. THERE'S NO WAY FOR YOU TO CONTROL ANOTHER PERSON'S THOUGHTS.

I once heard a man say that when he was in his 20s, he worried about what everyone thought of him. By the time he got into his 40s, he let go of the worry about other people, and it made his life much easier. He said when he got into his 60s, he learned the truth that was there the whole time: all the people he once worried about weren't thinking about him at all.

You may find it much easier to handle the problem once you know what the issue is. I can tell you that in my own life I struggled in this area for a very long time, until I finally came to realize what the issue was. I believe what I discovered may help you as well. And here it is: when people are worried about what others think of them, it is because they are seeking one simple thing from those people, whether they admit it or not. And this is the one thing they seek:

A - P - P - R - O - V - A - L

People want to be well spoken of, well thought of, well favored, accepted, acceptable. That's the bottom line. There is nothing necessarily wrong with that, unless you go to an extreme with your need for approval, and allow yourself to be paralyzed from taking action because you're afraid someone will not approve of you. In a nutshell, many people have "the cart before the horse," so to speak. They mistakenly believe that they can't feel good about themselves unless someone feels good about them first. Author Joyce Meyer has written extensively on this issue in her best-selling book "Approval Addiction: Overcoming Your Need To Please Everyone", as this was an issue she struggled with herself for many years. In Paul Coughlin's book, "No More Christian Nice Guy: When Being Nice Instead of Good Hurts Men, Women and Children," he states that the "disease to please" has prevented far too many males from fully living, and fully celebrating, the identity of complete manhood. Both books are excellent references for study, and I recommend them highly.

If however, you are not one given to investing time in such studies, there is a simple approach that may help you to overcome this challenge. Keep this in mind: it really doesn't matter who approves of you or does not approve of you, none of that matters unless you receive the approval of the one person on earth whose opinion in your life is superior to anyone else in existence, the only exception being the Creator Himself.

And that opinion belongs to the one and only YOU.

The only way someone's negative opinion of you can stop you in your tracks is if you agree with them, and in so doing turn those negative opinions onto yourself. So keep that in mind the next time you are tempted to allow the fear of man to put you (and keep you) in bondage. Their approval of you is not necessary, and you don't need their permission. They have the right to say anything they want about you, good bad or indifferent. And you have the right to disagree with everything they say about you, good bad or indifferent.

Let them say whatever they want. Have them talk about you, criticize you, laugh at you, lie on you, say whatever they want. You're not going to stop them, and you do not have to stop them, either.

You see, the only opinion of you that really counts, is yours.

Give yourself permission...give yourself favor...

Give yourself approval to do those things you've always wanted to do...

And let nothing, and let no one, hold you back...

Read it and reap...

Be blessed today...

And we'll talk again...

6. You Have Buried Treasure

In Russell Conwell's classic story "Acres of Diamonds," we are told of a man who sells his property for the sake of traveling the world in search of diamonds, only to find a sad end to his life, heartbroken and despondent, as he never finds what he seeks. As the original owner in vain sought his fortune elsewhere, the new owner was out surveying his property one day when he caught a glimpse of something sparkling in the sand at the edge of a stream. When he went to investigate, he discovered that the sparkling object was in fact, a diamond. A diamond which would lead the new owner to convert the property he purchased into a diamond mine. The treasure the original owner sought was his all along, but because he didn't take the time to learn its value, he sacrificed the fortune he already possessed for riches that would never become his.

If you believe that story has no significance in any way today, then please listen to what I'm about to say very carefully:

Just like the first owner in that story, so many people are throwing away their hidden treasures in search of imaginary riches. They think if they chase after some fantasy they'll make all their dreams come true. The sad fact is that in many cases, those people had the key to open their own personal vaults of wealth all along, both literally and figuratively. They just didn't take the time to "mine" the vein of gold that already was in their possession.

The best way to mine your own vein is to take stock of your buried treasure: gifts, talents and abilities you already possess. Don't get discouraged about this process. Too many people pay far too much attention to what negative people have to say about them and their talents. Often what others say about you and your talent is insulting, degrading, and just plain humiliating. You find yourself being accused by these pessimists of having no talent to speak of, when in truth those who disparage your abilities are envious, even jealous of what you can do, so the best response they can come up with in an effort to feel better about themselves is to try to convince you to doubt your capabilities. That's the only "talent" they have left because they gave up on their own abilities long ago.

Their own treasure remains buried, and as we have all heard before, "misery loves company."

I suggest you find people with which you share a sense of mutual respect for a more honest appraisal of your skills. These people have no ax to grind, and hold no grudge against you. You'll be pleasantly surprised to learn that many of them want to help you succeed, and would like nothing better than to have a hand in helping you get where you want to go in life. They may even have suggestions regarding ways you can best use your talents which you possibly hadn't before considered.

And where to find this buried treasure of which I speak? The best starting place is your own mirror, the mirror of your heart. You see, you need to recognize within yourself that you have value. You have capabilities the world is waiting patiently for you to display. You have a voice the world is longing to hear. There are people you have yet to meet, or to know, who are clamoring for you to take your rightful position in the world. Not many people care whether or not you make a living, but there are countless numbers of people today who are waiting to find out if you will, through your natural gifts, make a contribution, or better still, make a difference.

Don't worry about having to compete with, or compare yourself with others in an effort to display your talents. And don't believe the lie that life has passed you by. It hasn't. There is a place reserved just for you, only for you, which can be filled by no one but you:

"A man's gift makes room for him, and brings him before great men."
- Proverbs 18:16

It is in the use of your gifts, the display of your talents and abilities, that you can find true fulfillment, joy, and peace. This brings a sense of contentment and a clarity of purpose that words can scarcely begin to describe:

"This is the true joy in life, the being used for a purpose recognized by yourself as a mighty one; the being thoroughly worn out before you are thrown on the scrap heap; the being a force of Nature instead of a selfish feverish little clod of ailments and grievances complaining that the world will not devote itself to making you happy."
- George Bernard Shaw (1856-1950)

Think about your own life. Hasn't there been at least one time in your life when you used your abilities to reach out on the behalf of others, and found a sense of joy, fulfillment and satisfaction that words could barely describe? I believe that for some of you this may already be true. You've already made a difference is someone else's life. It makes no difference whether what you did was on a large or small scale. You made somebody's life better by standing up and stepping out on their behalf, and because of you, their life will never be the same.

So don't make the mistake of the original owner in Dr. Conwell's story. Take the time to learn of your own value. Find out where your talents lie. Use your gifts. Sharpen your skills. Make full use of the capabilities that reside within you. Seek out wisdom as to how you should mine the gold "vein" in your possession. And like the new property owner discovered, you too will learn that you don't have to go further than your own back yard to find the buried treasure you seek.

Read it and reap...

Be blessed...

And we'll talk again...

7. Opportunity Knocks

Opportunity:
1. An appropriate or favorable time or occasion
2. A situation or condition favorable for the attainment of a goal
3. A good position, chance, or prospect, as for success

If you've never seen the movie, "Pride of The Yankees," starring Gary Cooper and Teresa Wright, rent it as soon as you get the chance. It's so much more than just a baseball movie. It's a heartwarming, and heartbreaking story about Lou Gehrig, a man nicknamed “The Iron Horse.” He seemed to be indestructible, invincible. While facing the premature end to his life because of debilitating disease, he handled the situation with all the courage, dignity, and class he could muster.

But that's not why I recommend this movie. There are early scenes in the picture which I believe you should give close attention. These scenes describe his early years. His mother repeatedly told him of her dream for him to go to college and become and engineer, "just like [his] Uncle Otto," she repeatedly said.

Young Lou went along: "All right, Ma. Whatever you want me to be," he would reply.

But as he grew older, his desire to play baseball began to conflict with his mother's dream. In a later scene, a sportswriter and a baseball executive would approach him on the Columbia University baseball field (he was their starting first baseman), and talk to him about signing a professional contract with the New York Yankees. At first Lou is excited about the offer, but remembering his mother's wishes backs off, saying, "...but I'm going to be an engineer..."

His baseball talent could not be denied, however, and Lou did eventually sign with the Yankees, much to his mother's disappointment. While she was hurt that he had let her down by denying her dream for him, she did eventually come to respect him for making his own decision about how he should live his life. The rest of the movie reveals the importance of Lou making his own decisions in regarding his career, his marriage, and sadly, the situation previously mentioned which cut his life all too short.

Much can be learned from watching this movie about how to handle such potentially delicate and difficult situations. Sometimes we struggle in our own lives with opportunities presented to us. Not necessarily because the offer we receive is illegal, or immoral, or unethical. Not even because what we're asked to do is wrong. Most times there's nothing at all wrong with the opportunity we have been given. The big issue in many cases has to do with someone in our circle who does not see the big chance to succeed that we see. They may not agree, they may not approve. Or, as is so often the case, they don't agree because they had something else in mind for us to do, something conflicting with our desires, and they believe they know best how to handle our situation.

At least that's what seems to be true. But when the curtain is pulled back, much like Dorothy did in "The Wizard of Oz," the truth we find is usually quite a bit different. Often, what these people who "know what's best" are really doing is trying to use the lives of others as a way to relive theirs, so they can have a second chance to take advantage of some opportunities they may have had in their lives, but missed out on, whether through their own poor decisions, or those of someone else.

Allow me to clarify, and please think about this carefully:

You show me someone who's trying to plan your life, and I'll show you someone who has no plan for their own life. They're just going through the motions. Their plan, their dream, their goal, their main objective in life is to live their life, THROUGH YOU.

It's a vicious cycle that needs to stop. And for you the buck must stop here. The answer to this dilemma is not easy, but it is simple. it can be summed up in four words:

EXERCISE YOUR FREE WILL

The people in your midst may not like or agree with your choices. But you need to realize that when issues of health, safety, or risk of loss (especially of life) do not factor into the equation (and they often don't) the only choice they really have, much like Lou Gehrig's disappointed mother, is to realize they must respect your decision. Whether they like it or not, whether they agree with it or not, they must respect it, and you.

Changing your mind is not their job, and changing their mind is not your job, either. You can agree to disagree. The Apostle Paul speaks plainly about "...putting off childish things," when it's time to grow up and become a (wo)man. Sadly there are far too many people of adult age alive today who have yet to even consider cutting those childhood bonds loose and taking on the mantle of maturity in adulthood.

But that's their problem, not yours.

So the next time you are presented with an opportunity to better your own life, and the naysayers in your midst want to wail and howl about how you're making a big mistake, be respectful of them, their opinions, and feelings. Then make the decision that works best for you. In Psalms God promises that as you delight yourself in Him, He will give you the desires of YOUR heart, not theirs. So make the decision that will bring peace to your heart and to your life, and allow them to respond according to the dictates of their own conscience.

And always remember, it's not just in a car commercial that you hear someone say,

"It's Opportunity here. And I'm knocking."

When Opportunity knocks again, will you answer...?

Read it and reap...

Be blessed today...

And we'll talk again...

8. Remember...Who You Are...

Exile: a period of prolonged separation, usually by force, from one's native land, country, or home

Do you feel like you are experiencing a time of exile in your life? Have been dreams been dashed by disappointment? Have you been robbed of a sense of purpose? Stung by setbacks? Traumatized by tragedy? If this describes you in any way, then take heart. Be of good courage, don't be afraid or dismayed. There is still a chance for you to turn things around in your life. There is a light at the end of the tunnel. Let me show you what I mean.

You may know the story of the Disney movie "The Lion King." Simba, young prince and heir to the throne occupied by his father Mufasa, is thrown into his own exile, barely escaping with his life after his father is murdered and his throne seized by Scar, Mufasa's brother and Simba's uncle. Simba grows into adulthood, but cannot escape his grief or the guilt of his past, as he mistakenly believes, thanks to Scar's lies, that he is responsible for his father's death.

In the midst of his grief, despair and growing sense of hopelessness Simba has an encounter which alters his life, and puts him back on track toward fulfilling his destiny. During a storm he sees a vision in the approaching clouds. It is his father Mufasa calling to him with a most urgent message.

Reprimanding Simba for forgetting his heritage and his lineage ("you have forgotten who you are and so, have forgotten me"), he restores Simba to his rightful position ("look inside yourself; you are more than what you have become; you must take your place in the circle of life..."), and he reminds Simba of his right standing ("...remember who you are..." "...you are my son, and the one true king..."). As he leaves, Mufasa's words echo in Simba's ears in a final reminder as the storm clouds recede from the sky:

REMEMBER...WHO YOU ARE...
REMEMBER...REMEMBER...REMEMBER...

Once his eyes were opened, Simba returned to his homeland to confront his past and the uncle who manipulated him with guilt and lies to steal his throne. Despite some conflict along the way, including one final attempt by Scar to shame him with the guilt of his past in the eyes of his pride, he is able to overcome his uncle's opposition and take his place as the king and leader he was always destined to be.

If you are reading this and recognize yourself as someone experiencing a time of exile in your own life, then realize it is just as possible for you, in the midst of your despair, to get your situation and your life turned completely around. Even in the middle of your storm you need to understand that your problems are not permanent; they are not designed to last. Like the clouds that confronted Simba, the storm clouds you see can only dissipate once they have run their course.

"Therefore we do not become discouraged (utterly spiritless, exhausted, and wearied out through fear)...For our light, momentary affliction (this slight distress of the passing hour) is ever more and more abundantly preparing and producing and achieving for us and everlasting weight of glory [beyond all measure, excessively surpassing all comparisons and all calculations, a vast and transcendent glory and blessedness never to

cease!], Since we consider and look not to the things that are seen but to the things that are unseen; for the things that are visible are temporal (brief and fleeting), but the things that are invisible are deathless and everlasting."
- II Corinthians 5:16-18 Amplified Bible

No matter what you face right now, no matter how impossible it seems, you have a place reserved just for you. You have a rightful position that no one can take away from you, no matter how hard they try. Your identity is unique; there is no one in history who is capable to doing what you have the capacity to accomplish. There is room, and there is time, for you to fulfill the destiny you have been brought into the world to complete. Not only that, there are people in this world who are waiting for the opportunity to see what happens when you complete the assignment you have been given as you make your life's journey:

"A man's gift makes room for him and brings him before great men." - Proverbs 18:16

So please allow me to encourage you. Take your place at the table of life. Invitations have already been sent, and one of them has your name on it.

You are qualified to attend, you cannot be turned away. And best of all, everyone at the table wants you to be there. Yes, you. They cannot wait to see you. Because they know that without you, life wouldn't be as good as it could possibly be. You may ask, but what about my past? Realize that everyone has a past, and everyone has been hurt in their past at one time or another. But also realize that until you stop running from your past and start learning from it, you will not be able to overcome the hurt, the pain, the anger, and the heartache of your past to experience the joy, the peace, the contentment that can be achieved.

And should you feel any pangs of doubt about your standing, about your worthiness, about your right to take your place at the table of life, be encouraged as Simba was, by Mufasa's final exhortation from on high:

REMEMBER WHO YOU ARE
...REMEMBER...REMEMBER...REMEMBER....

Read it and reap...

Be blessed...

And we'll talk again...

9. One of a Kind

On December 15, 1966 Walter Elias "Walt" Disney, creator of Mickey Mouse and Donald Duck, cartoon characters that inspired him to create Disneyland, "The Happiest Place on Earth", died of lung cancer just 10 days after his 65th birthday. Many tributes that flowed as news of his death spread all over the world, but one above all best summed up The Great Imagineer's legacy:

"He was an original. Not just an American original, but an original. Period." - MousePlanet.com

It was said that while he lay in the hospital on what would become his deathbed, he invited visitors at his bedside to look up at the ceiling with him. That would seem a strange request, except for the fact that Walt wanted to show his visitors the plans for a dream he knew he would not live to see come true. For on that ceiling he placed the designs for a family attraction that in 1971 would be opened to the public as Walt Disney World.

Disney was recognized for his many innovations

in animation and theme park design. The Walt Disney Studios were known for groundbreaking advancements in animation and cinematography, as the 3D style animations in his feature length cartoons often gave the appearance of life-like drama. Live action models acted out the scenes of Walt's films for the benefit of his animators, who interpreted the scenes depicted by the models into cartoon form.

For his work, Walt Disney received 59 Academy Award nominations, winning 26 such awards, more than any man or woman in motion picture history, including winning four Academy Awards in a single year, also more than anyone in history. Disney also received seven Emmy Awards for television excellence. His name is associated with theme parks and resorts in the United States, Japan, France, and China.

In the midst of all the accolades he received during his lifetime, Walt never lost his sense of perspective. Disney habitually made it a point to remind everyone who worked with him to transform his enterprise into an empire, that they should never ever forget, "...it all started with a mouse."

In fact, it was during a time of great adversity for him, after having endured a failed business and bankruptcy, that his fortunes turned permanently for the better. On a train ride to California with only $40 in his pocket, he created a character that would become his partner in success for life. He got the idea for this character from raising a pet mouse during his earlier days in the Midwest. Originally called Mortimer, Walt's wife insisted that he change the character's name to give it what she believed would be a kinder, more appealing identity: Mickey. The rest, as they say, is history.

Disney lived only 65 years, but what a life it was. He packed so much into his lifetime, he made an impact that would last for generations, one that remains to this day. Animation, cinema, music, entertainment, television, amusement, and even sports owe Walt a huge debt of gratitude, as his life had a major influence on American society, and on mankind as a whole.

So, you must be wondering after reading this story, what any of this has to do with you? I'm glad you asked. Like Walt Disney, you were designed to be One of a Kind, an individual whose place in history has never before existed.

Without your contribution, history will not be as special, or as unique, as it can truly become.

You see, Genesis 1:26 says God made man in His image, after His likeness. One of God's major attributes is the ability to CREATE. Ephesians 5:1 says we should be followers of God. The word "followers" in that verse means "imitators". When we were kids we gave a certain name to people who mimicked us. We called them "copycats". In that sense, God expects us, as His creation, to "copycat" Him, so to speak. He is the only one whose nature, whose character, we are supposed to reflect. As some people would say, as His child we should "take after" Him. The real issue, it appears, is that we get ourselves all tied up in knots because we think we should be like other people. Walk like, talk like, think like, be like, somebody else who (like the rest of us) was created in God's image, after God's likeness, whether they want to admit it or not.

Like everyone else that has ever lived, including Walt Disney, you were born on purpose, for a purpose. There is a role for you to play in life that no one can fulfill like you can. There is a place in the puzzle board of life where only you can fit.

There is an impact that only you can make in this world. Other people may be able to do things that are similar to what you can do, but nobody can do what you can do, EXACTLY the way that you do it. (In the 1960s, Motown recording artists The Temptations performed a song that spoke of an individual's uniqueness. It was called "The Way You Do The Things You Do". While they may have been singing about an entirely different subject, the principle is very much the same. Give it a listen on YouTube and find out for yourself) Without you, life on this earth would not as good as it could possibly be.

If you've ever seen the movie, "It's A Wonderful Life", with Jimmy Stewart and Donna Reed (a Christmas classic; if you have never seen it, buy it, rent it, TiVo it, DVR it; whatever you need to do, watch that movie!), I'm sure you remember the part of the movie where Jimmy Stewart's character, George Bailey, gets a chance to see what life would be like if he'd never been born. He got to see firsthand all the heartache, tragedy, and broken lives that would have resulted had he not been alive to intervene on the behalf of so many. At the end of the movie, when the people of Bedford Falls propose a toast in his honor, led by

George's younger brother Harry, he is proclaimed, "...the richest man in town." None of that would have been possible if George hadn't been around to play his very special part. Watch the movie and see for yourself.

But that just was a movie. A motion picture. Nothing but family entertainment. Surely that can't represent reality, can it? Listen, there is truth in the saying, "life imitates art". That fine piece of cinema from director Frank Capra was not a fantasy, it was an example to all of us. Like George Bailey, you have a special role to play in life. You have an impact to make in life like no one else can. In fact, if you read scripture you will discover that God has some very interesting things to say about the importance of your individual identity. For instance:

"Now you [collectively] are Christ's body and [individually] you are members of it, each part severally and distinct [each with its own place and function]."
- I Corinthians 12:27 Amplified Bible

If you read the entire 12th chapter of the book of I Corinthians, you will discover that the writer (the Apostle Paul) talks about the members of the body of Christ as if they were members of a human body, from a symbolic perspective. The point he makes is very simple. He says there is no part of the body that can look at another part and declare that part to be unnecessary, just because it was designed to perform a different function. All parts play an important function, or as the scripture says, "...every joint supplieth" (Ephesians 4:16)

Put in financial terms, it's like this: we spend too much time appreciating the value of others; at the same time we spend too much time depreciating the value we have ourselves. We don't recognize the value in the gifts that we have because we assume we are supposed to do what someone else is doing, we assume that their gifts are so much better than ours, and that our gifts should resemble theirs, otherwise something is wrong. We try to make people our example instead of God, and that is a recipe for disaster. Man was never intended to be a standard unto himself. Remember God made man after HIS image, not man's image. Without God, man has no image to pattern himself after.

“Not that we [have the audacity to] venture to class or [even to] compare ourselves with some who exalt and furnish testimonials for themselves! However, when they measure themselves with themselves and compare themselves with one another, they are without understanding and behave unwisely. However, let him who boasts and glories boast and glory in the Lord. For it is not [the man] who praises and commends himself who is approved and accepted, but [it is the person] whom the Lord accredits and commends." - II Corinthians 10:12,17-18 Amplified Bible

You see, it is God who gives you the ability to make an impact. NOT YOU. To grovel in the dirt in an attempt to be "humble" for fear that using the gifts you've been given by God will make you "arrogant" somehow, is just as bad as taking the gifts God has given you and boasting of them before men, heaping praise upon yourself for all you have accomplished, when it is God who has positioned you to make the impact you are able to make while you walk this earth. In either case, the focus is not on God, it's on YOU.

So what more is there to be said? You need to realize that you have just as important a place in this earth as anyone who has ever lived. You have a very important part to play, some very big shoes to fill (don't worry, they're yours), and you have a place of honor that is reserved only for you, and no one else. You have a starring role on the earth, just like everyone else. Only in the sense that God gets top billing, are you considered a supporting actor or actress. But it's up to you to make the best of the role you have been given to play:

"However, we possess this precious treasure [the divine Light of the Gospel] in [frail, human] vessels of earth, that the grandeur and exceeding greatness of the power may be shown to be from God and not from ourselves." - II Corinthians 4:7 Amplified Bible

"But in a great house there are not only vessels of gold and silver, but also [utensils] of wood and earthenware, and some for honorable and noble [use] and some for menial and ignoble [use]. So whoever cleanses himself [from what is ignoble and unclean, who separates himself from contaminating and corrupting influences] will [them himself] be a vessel set apart and useful for honorable and noble purposes, consecrated and

profitable to the Master, fit and ready for any good work." - II Timothy 2:20,21 Amplified Bible

You see, it is up to you to decide if you're going to use the God given gifts, talents and abilities within you to make an impact. You have a free will, so you are free to put these attributes into motion any time you choose. Or you can choose not to. Remember though, that you have your own unique path to walk, your own trail to blaze. It is not your destiny to ride someone else's coattails. Dr. Myles Munroe lamented in his book, "In Pursuit of Purpose", that "...too many people are born original, but die as copies."

So pursue your own unique role. You may not make the impact on the world that Walt Disney made. Or maybe you'll make a bigger one, who can say? One thing is for sure. Only one person can influence your corner of the globe in such a way as to transform the place where you now stand into a little slice of Heaven.

AND THAT ONE PERSON IS YOU. TRULY YOU ARE...

ONE OF A KIND.

Read it and reap...

Be blessed...

And we'll talk again...

10. Know That Your Life Is Important

"A life is not important, except in the impact is has on other lives."
- Jackie Robinson (1919-1972)

"I assure you, most solemnly I tell you, Unless a grain of wheat falls into the earth and dies, it remains [just one grain; it never becomes more but lives] by itself alone. But if it dies, it produces many others and yields a rich harvest."
- John 12:24

Your life does not become important until you take action to impact, influence, and positively affect other lives. Your life becomes significant when you treat others as if they themselves are living significant lives. One of the best examples of such truth can be found in the classic movie, "It's A Wonderful Life," whose main character, George Bailey, is played by legendary Academy Award winning actor Jimmy Stewart. Throughout his life, George is continually making a difference for others, from the time he rescued his brother Harry from drowning, to the time he prevented the local druggist (called a pharmacist today) from making a potentially fatal mistake with a prescription that would have poisoned a child, to keeping the local Building and Loan company from going under when his father suddenly and unexpectedly died, to helping make his hometown, Bedford Falls, a safe, affordable community for families who might not have otherwise been able to own their own homes.

George throughout his life was making a major difference in the lives of so many people, touching many hearts, but because of personal setbacks and hardships, he was unable to see and appreciate the positive results. Then in a strange twist that would be later immortalized by Rod Serling in a television series that would one day become "The Twilight Zone," George is offered the rare opportunity to see how different planet earth would have been had he never been born. He saw life without his existence, without his participation. As he was given the chance to see how stark in contrast the people and places of his hometown would have been without him around to influence it, George was given what we in today's world would call a "reality check":

"George, you've really had a wonderful life. Wouldn't it be a shame to just throw it all away?"

He was so moved by the images he had seen, the trauma and trouble he'd been privileged to witness that far outweighed and overshadowed whatever discomfort and distress he was facing, George found himself at the edge of a bridge he originally considered using to end what he once considered his "sorry existence," his tragic lot in life, begging and pleading to have his life back. He didn't care what happened to him any more, he just wanted to live again.

Once he realized he'd been given the chance to reclaim his life, he embraced it fully, he embraced it joyfully, complete with all the the challenges, all the problems, and yes, even the trouble. All of it. As he did so, he was unexpectedly blessed by so many people whose lives he had impacted over the years, culminating in a toast proposed by his brother Harry in a year end celebration, the same brother he had rescued from drowning during their childhood. It turned out to be a most fitting and proper declaration to honor a man who had given so much of himself to positively influence the lives of so many people in the town he loved and claimed for his own: *"...to my brother George: the richest man in town..."*

If I've left any gaps in this story, I recommend you rent this movie, or better yet, buy the movie to watch over and over again to fully comprehend the message of this classic film. It may touch your life in more ways than you could possibly know.

That being said, I urge you, I beseech you, I beg you: don't wait until the end of your days to realize that despite what you're facing right now, you had the chance to live a life more wonderful and magnificent than anyone could possibly have imagined, but because of faulty perceptions and misconceptions you squandered it. Unlike the movie there is no Rewind button. Your seconds, minutes, hours, days, weeks, months, years, your very life is constantly on the Play button. Even when you think it's on Pause, it is always in motion.

So embrace the people, the places, the things with which you have been presented. Drink in all that life has to offer. And bless and refresh those with whom you come in contact along the way.

Make your life significant.

Make your life have impact.

Make your life have influence.

And like Jackie Robinson and George Bailey discovered,

KNOW THAT YOUR LIFE IS IMPORTANT

Read it and reap...

Be blessed today...

And we'll talk again...

11. Love Yourself As Your Neighbor

"And you shall love the Lord your God with all your heart, with all your soul, with all your mind, and with all your strength. This is the first commandment. And the second, like it, is this: You shall love your neighbor as yourself. There is no other commandment greater than these." - Mark 12:30,31

When I was a child, one of my favorite television programs was The Three Stooges. (Some may debate that I'm still in my childhood, but I digress) One of the reasons I enjoyed the show so much, besides the fact that there was so much physical comedy (it was called "slapstick" back in those days) with the eye gouging, falling from ladders, and hitting each other over the head with whatever tools they could find (usually hammers, in a "kids, don't try this at home" fashion), was the fact that they seemed very comfortable in their own skin, and had no problem poking fun at themselves, while at the same time never putting others down. It was good clean fun, such as it was, and in the end nobody really got hurt. A common theme in their shows was the trio finding themselves in a situation where they'd rub elbows with people at "high society" gatherings, where strangely (to them, at least) they found themselves welcome, easily fitting in among the crowd, because they looked to be on equal footing with the other guests, even down to the tuxedos they would wear. During the festivities the punch line would always be the same: someone would approach them and address them with the standard greeting: "GENTLEMEN...!!!!" Startled, the three would look all around the room, trying to find the individual who was being addressed, not realizing the greeting was intended for them, and immediately respond, "WHERE??????"

As a child, I would laugh at that exchange, because the intended result was to get a few chuckles from the audience. But as I have grown up since that time, I have given that scene I witnessed many times a great deal of thought. While in a short film, the motivation was humorous, and successfully so, the reality in today's world is that we have people who, like the Stooges, have a faulty, even flawed sense of their identity.

As I write this in 2010, I witness that we as mankind have lost an appreciation for the value of human life.

That there is even a debate as to whether an unborn child is a living being, a living soul, is a notion that would have astounded people of prior generations as to the reality of its possibility. And what of the people who walk this planet today? What about their value? Don't we all have something of worth to contribute as we walk out our lives across this stage we call earth? If you listen to certain people speak, you would think some are useless refuse, only good for being discarded like the gum (or objects less appealing) that attach themselves to the bottom of our shoes. The Creator of the Universe has a somewhat different view, however. This is what He has to say about mankind:

"Before I formed you in the womb I knew and approved of you [as My chosen instrument]..." - Jeremiah 1:5

"For you did form my inward parts; You did knit me together in my mother's womb. I will praise You, for I am fearfully and wonderfully made..." - Psalm 139:13,14

"Then God said, Let Us make man in Our image, according to Our likeness...

So God created man in His own image...male and female He created them.
Then God blessed them, and God said to them, Be fruitful and multiply;
And God said, See I have given you every herb that yields seed which is on the face of the earth, and every tree whose fruit yields seed; to you it shall be for food.
Also, to every beast of the earth, to every bird of the air, and to everything that creeps on the earth, in which there is life, I have given every green herb for food; and it was so.
Then God saw everything that He had made, and indeed it was very good."*
*- Genesis 1:27-31 (*including man)*

When I read these passages and others like them in scripture I cannot help but believe that God saw us as valuable to Him when we were created. So much so that He made provision for us before we existed. He even put us in charge of the whole operation on earth. The problem, I believe, is that we have not followed His example and recognized the value He sees in us as the high point of His creation. We have divided ourselves, squabbled, quarreled, and fought amongst ourselves, even killed ourselves.

We have drawn lines in the sand between ourselves, trying to make ourselves better (or worse) than someone who appears different than we believe we are. It seems that once dominion of earth was lost, we have since that day tried to regain it by exercising dominion over each other.

On the other side of the coin we have people who grovel at the feet of others, trying to curry their favor. We idolize some people and demonize others. Sometimes we even demonize ourselves. We think so little of our own value that we worship other people in an effort to feel good about ourselves. We talk about gifts, talents, and abilities that belong to others, but refuse to recognize the ones God has given us. We're just like the Stooges in their comedies who say, "Where?" when someone takes the time to recognize the gifts and talents in us that we blind ourselves to. So, what's the solution? Here's what I propose:

LOVE YOURSELF AS YOUR NEIGHBOR

I can see some of you reading this and saying, "But doesn't scripture tell us to love our neighbor as ourselves?"

You're right, it does. But here's the reality:

Too many people love their neighbors, but not themselves. We do things for others we would never consider doing for ourselves. We "bend over backwards", as it were, to serve other people in ways we would consider extravagant or extreme if we were to even contemplate those same things being done on our own behalf, or if we were to "bless ourselves" in like fashion. As a teenager growing up on Long Island, my Pastor at that time, Gene Profeta, made a startling statement, which years later makes perfect sense. He told us, "The Bible says to love your neighbor AS yourself, NOT BETTER THAN YOURSELF." I can truly say I am guilty of doing the opposite of what he suggested, as are some of you.

It is not an act of arrogance to recognize your talents. It is an acknowledgment of the Greater One that lives in you, the Most High God who gave you those gifts and talents in the first place. Too many of us put ourselves down and call it being "humble", failing to realize that to treat yourself in this manner is to also put down the One who took the time to form you, fashion you, fearfully and wonderfully make you.

To insult the gift is to insult the Giver. Don't believe me? In your next time of "humility", ask yourself this: are you focused on God, or on yourself? Think about it.

The arrogance comes when you flaunt the gifts and talents you have in the face of others, as if you had something to do with acquiring those gifts, talents, and abilities you possess, and God did not. Recognizing Him is not arrogance, but recognizing yourself at God's expense, is. Back in the day, prior generations said, "Remember where you came from". At that saying relates to the Creator of the Universe, those words could not ring more true.

With all this said, I humbly suggest to you that you take the time to recognize the gifts, the talents, the abilities, and most of all, recognize the value, that the Creator has placed inside of you. Please do so if you truly want to love your neighbor, because you cannot give to others what you do not first have yourself.

So the next time someone calls you by name, the next time someone blesses you, the next time someone addresses you in the manner to which you are truly endowed and entitled, unlike the Stooges, you will be able to acknowledge their greeting properly, and address them with the appropriate blessing, endowment, and entitlement in return.

Love on yourself with the love of the Most High God. Recognize and believe the love which God has in His heart for you. Then with that heart full of the love of God, go to your neighbor:

"And as you would like and desire that men would do to you, do exactly so to them."
- Luke 6:31 Amplified Bible

Read it and reap...

Be blessed...

We'll talk again....

12. There's Power In Your Tongue

"There are those who speak rashly, like the piercing of a sword, but the tongue of the wise brings healing." - Proverbs 12:18, Amplified Bible

In the Random House Webster's Collegiate Dictionary you will find these definitions for words:

1. a unit of language that functions as a principal carrier of meaning
2. verbal expression, esp. speech or talk
3. contentious or angry speech, a quarrel
4. an authoritative utterance or command

Words are a powerful force which can be used for good or evil, blessing or cursing, health or harm. When used properly words can be a wellspring of life; improper use can cause death and destruction as a root of bitterness springs forth.

"How forceful are right words." - Job 6:25

"A word fitly spoken and in due season is like apples of gold in settings of silver."
- Proverbs 25:11

"A man has joy in making an apt answer, and a word spoken at the right moment--how good it is!" - Proverbs 15:23

"A soft answer turns away wrath, but grievous words stir up anger."
- Proverbs 15:1

"A fool vents all his feelings, but a wise man holds them back."
- Proverbs 29:11

"Do you see a man hasty in his words? There is more hope for a fool than for him."
- Proverbs 29:20

The right words at the right time can lift a downcast spirit. The wrong words, recklessly spoken, can crush the joy and suck the life out of even the happiest soul. People throughout history have established or wrecked families, businesses, relationships, jobs, careers, marriages, friendships, governments, even their very lives, based on the power which was applied or misapplied, used or abused, through the words they spoke, whether intentional or unintentional. For better or worse, people have literally been "hung" by their tongue.

"Death and life are in the power of the tongue, and they who indulge in it shall eat the fruit of it [for death or life]." - Proverbs 18:21

"You are snared with the words of your lips, you are caught by the speech of your mouth."
- Proverbs 6:2

Words can be creative, words can be destructive. But even in those times when words have been spoken in haste, resulting in emotional damage due to rash, harsh, even abusive callousness, words can be used in a redemptive manner, as a healing balm to salve even the most painful wound. And this can be achieved, no matter how deeply harsh words may have cut.

"For I will restore health to you, and heal you of your wounds, says the Lord..."
- Jeremiah 30:17

"Praise the Lord! For it is good to sing praises to our God, for He is gracious and lovely: praise is becoming and appropriate. He heals the brokenhearted and binds up their wounds [curing their pains and their sorrows]. - Psalms 147:1,3

What more can I say of these things? Only this:

If there are people in your life that you hold near and dear to your heart, make time at every opportunity you have with them to acknowledge them, applaud them, appreciate them, bless them, encourage them, celebrate them, support them, inspire them, and most of all love them.
And if there are people you have hurt, even slightly, it may not be too late to redeem those lost relationships if you dare to use the power of the right words to salve, and even possibly heal those wounds with grace and humility. Life is too short and time on earth is too precious to waste holding grudges.

"Let your speech always be with grace, seasoned with salt, that you may know how you ought to answer each one." - Colossians 4:6

The choice is yours. Will you use your words for life or death? Blessing or cursing? Good or evil?

The power is in your tongue.

Read it and reap...

Be blessed...

And we'll talk again...

13. Stand Up To The Bullies In Your Life

Bully: a quarrelsome, overbearing person who badgers and intimidates smaller or weaker people; a loudly arrogant individual

"A bully is someone who exposes your faults in an attempt to cover up his own." - Rev. Gene Profeta

Many of you are familiar with bullies. You, or someone you know, may have been the victim of a bully during your childhood, your school days, or both. Most people think of the "big, bad bully" at the schoolyard that everyone was afraid of, nobody would speak to, and absolutely NO ONE wanted to get on the bad side of, aka the "hit" list (meaning the bully is the Hitter, and you are the "Hittee", the target of the bully's wrath).

Sometimes bullies weren't on the schoolyard. They could be found in your neighborhood, for instance. No matter where they could be found, every bully seeks to embarrass you, humiliate you, intimidate you, or manipulate you for one very basic reason: they want to control you. But don't assume that bullying is something you outgrow once you leave childhood.

That isn't the least bit true, not by a longshot. You see, bullies can be found in many places. On the athletic field. In a conference room. In a grocery store. On the highway (ever heard of road rage?). At the beach (sand kicking in the face ring a bell?). In a gym. On the ski slopes. A movie theater. A parking lot. An apartment building. A bank. And other places. So many places.

These encounters don't often happen with so many people. Often it's no more than a remnant of people who badger others with their bullying tendencies. But sadly, the most painful encounters occur as we grow older, often as the result of interactions with the people who profess to care about us the most. Your parents. Your spouse. Your in-laws. Your siblings. Your relatives. Many who fall into these categories do so without realizing what they are doing. Others are fully aware that they do so. But they all do their bullying just like the rest for much the same reason:

BECAUSE THEY WANT TO IMPOSE OR ENFORCE THEIR WILL UPON YOU

But what's really tough about this particular brand of bullying is that it often comes with some sort of threat, whether veiled or direct. It is a threat that states if you do not comply with their wishes, they will take something from you that is precious to you, valuable to you, near and dear to your heart. Often they will give you things with an ulterior motive, combined with a threat: "I gave you all this, and if you cross me, then I can take it away from you, which would leave you with nothing. Then what will you do without me to help you?"

Bullies of all shapes and sizes want to gain power and mastery over their victims.** They want their victims to believe that they are paralyzed, weak, and helpless in comparison to their tormentors. The reason why bullies would do this may astound you, but it is still true. Many people believe bullies have a strong self image, but as Rev. Profeta so eloquently stated, when you get past all the bellowing, all the bluff, and all of the bluster, bullies in reality are weak and helpless themselves, scared, frightened, and altogether powerless. (What they hope you never realize is that once you stand up to them, they'll back down.)

They see intimidation as a way to get attention. In their minds, it is not only the best way, it is the only way, because they are too afraid to try anything else. Bullies often have such a poor self-image that they believe in order to put themselves in high places they must bring others down to their level or lower. And for all their threats of abandoning you, in truth, bullies are afraid that one day the tables will be turned, and that you will leave them instead as soon as you have the opportunity to do so. This is why they seek to keep you down. But here's a paradox. By trying to hold onto people by dominating them, bullies achieve the opposite effect: they push people away. So in effect, by bullying, the very thing that bullies fear would happen comes to their doorstep. They create their own reality by driving people away from their presence.

Now, if you have ever been bullied, even if you are being bullied at this very moment, and you're fed up with being traumatized in this manner, whether you're a child or an adult, there are ways to stand up to bullies, and prevent this from becoming (or from continuing to be) an issue in your life. Here's what I suggest that you do:

1. TAKE YOUR POWER BACK

Bullies are all about power and control. They want you to believe that they are the source of everything good in your life. So you need to find strength in areas of your life that have absolutely nothing to do with what your would-be tormentor says or does. Find something to do that brings you joy and pleasure in life, something that in no way requires the involvement, or the approval, or anyone who would seek to control your life.

2. BUILD YOUR OWN TEAM OF ALLIES

Link up with like-minded people who care about you, support you, and love you as your are, F.A.A. (Flaws And All). These are the people who value you, appreciate, celebrate, applaud, validate you, and refuse to pass judgment against you. Any time they need to criticize, it is constructive, not condemning, because they believe in you, and will do whatever they can to help you. This team is a crucial asset for you to have in your arsenal, because one of the bully's tactics to gain power over you is to isolate you as much as is humanly possible. There truly is strength in numbers, so gather as much strength as you can. Friendship is a team sport.

"A friend loves at all times, and as a brother, is born for adversity." - Proverbs 17:17

3. UNDERSTAND THAT THE BULLY'S HANGUPS AND ISSUES BELONG TO THE BULLY, NOT TO YOU

Know this for a fact: you are not the cause of your tormentor's problems. Whatever issues they may have were in play long before you came on the scene. If they need help they should seek it, but that in no way makes you responsible for providing it. Oftentimes a bully seeks a scapegoat for heartache and anguish suffered earlier in life, and you just happen to be a convenient target. Stop accepting the blame for hurts, slights, and injuries inflicted by people in the bully's past that you don't know, and will likely never meet.

While it is true that a big part of your life here on earth involves making a positive impact in the lives of others, this does not make you responsible for causing others to achieve happiness in their lives. That ball has always been in their court, and that will never change. So decide today that you will not be their victim.

Stand up to the bullies that try to plague you with their misery, and dare to take steps in the direction of your own dreams for a change.

"I have learned that if one advances confidently in the direction of his dreams, and endeavors to live the life he has imagined, he will meet with success unexpected in common hours."
- Henry David Thoreau (1817-1862)

"Most folks are as happy as they make up their minds to be."
- Abraham Lincoln (1809-1865)

Read it and reap everyone...

Be blessed today...

And we'll talk again...

*(**"Bullies Looking for Reward, Psychologists Say", Washington Examiner http://www.washingtonexaminer.com/local/Bullies-looking-for-reward_-psychologists-say-92551809.html)*

14. Crabs In A Barrel

Did you know that when crabbers place in a barrel the crabs they have caught, they never have to worry about the crabs getting away? Did you know they are absolutely certain the crabs will not get away, even though the barrel is often left uncovered? That doesn't seem to make a lot of sense, unless you know a thing or two about crabs.

You see, when crabs find themselves in a barrel, a remarkable phenomenon takes place. If one crab is placed in a barrel, it will find its way out of the barrel with no trouble at all. But if two or more crabs are in that same barrel, all the crabs inside the barrel will die. I know that doesn't seem possible, but it is true. Here's why: crabs in a barrel will automatically latch onto each other, holding themselves firmly in place. If a crab is somehow able to make its way toward the top of the barrel to get up and out, the rest of the crabs will grab its claws with their own, and hold it in place until the "renegade" crab gives up its struggle and stays with the rest of its fellow crustaceans in group-imposed lockdown.

There are some people who hear the Crabs in a Barrel story and want to split hairs over minor details in the story:

Who put the crabs in the bucket? Why don't the crabs on top get out of the way so the crabs on the bottom can move up to the top? This one takes the cake: The crabs on top represent rich people, and the crabs on the bottom are poor people trying to get ahead but the rich people keep the poor people down...blah, blah, blah....

WHO CARES HOW THEY GOT THERE??????
DOES IT REALLY MATTER??????

Those arguments are irrelevant, irrelative, and immaterial. They have absolutely nothing to do with the heart of the issue, and they are posed by people who believe that someone other than themselves is, or should always be, responsible for their well-being. They don't party unless there's pity. They want no part of misery unless they have company to make them feel better about being miserable. And to paraphrase George Bernard Shaw, they believe the world is obligated to devote itself to making them happy.

(Here's something to consider: could these be the people of whom Booker T. Washington once spoke, that constantly parade their grievances in the public square to: a. get sympathy, and b. get paid? Just a thought.)

In reality, nothing could be further from the truth. The real issue has nothing to do with what's going on outside of us. And believe it or not, the issue has nothing to do with what has happened to us. The real issue, the real difference between success and failure, victory and defeat, winning and losing, is what takes place inside of us. Simply put, WHATCHA GONNA DO 'BOUT IT?? Austrian psychiatrist, psychotherapist, and World War II Holocaust survivor Viktor Frankl (1905-1997) wrote:

"The one thing you can't take away from me is the way I choose to respond to what you do to me. The last of one's freedoms is to choose one's attitude in any given circumstance."

This statement flies in the face of conventional beliefs that state how someone "made" us mad, sad, glad, bad, etc.

First Lady and United Nations ambassador Eleanor Roosevelt (1884-1962) may have said it best when she said, *"Nobody can make you feel inferior without your consent."*

What people don't want to see is that contrary to popular opinion, there are people who do overcome their situation. These "crabs" escape from their "bucket", so to speak. They make the changes necessary in their own lives which allow them to enjoy success in spite of the obstacles they face, while other "crabs" do not. These people develop as they age, while others simply age while refusing to develop.

WHY????

Most people will tell you it's all about fear. Some people are courageous, they take action, they are bold, they are fearless, hence, they are successful. Supposedly those people who don't make things happen are too fearful, too "chicken", to step out on faith and take a risk to make things happen. At least that's what we've been told. But is that really true? Many of us have heard of people who have taken action in spite of feeling any fear.

As Joyce Meyer often says, they "...do it afraid." So if it isn't fear, what could it possibly be? I submit to you that there is a force even more powerful than fear, a force that stops people dead in their tracks. Without this force, fear loses much of its potency, even much of its power to torment, to anguish, to mentally torture.

This force is defined as follows:

1. a feeling of uncertainty
2. distrust or suspicion
3. a situation causing uncertainty, or
4. just plain old unbelief

In case you haven't guessed by now what I'm talking about, let me spell it out for you:

D - O - U - B - T

Just like the crabs in the barrel trying to hold on for dear life, people in your midst will try to hold you back, because they don't believe they can succeed in the real world, and they don't believe you can succeed in the real world, either. They believe that any attempts you make to improve your lot in life will ultimately fail, so they try to "protect you" from setbacks, hurts, and other disappointments. What they don't see is that they are really preventing you from enjoying success, fulfillment, and joy, and that the overcoming of setbacks, hurts, disappointments, and challenges is part of the process of achieving success, fulfillment, and ultimately joy. They've allowed life and its challenges to short-circuit their zest for life, and in turn they are trying to short-circuit your enthusiasm for life and zest for living, whether they realize it or not. They have settled for less in life, and in so doing have mistaken short-term security for long-term success.

What they (and YOU) need to realize is that nothing in your life is going to change for the better until you do. Don't be one of those people who sit around waiting for a harvest before they think about sowing any seeds. That's like waiting to get paid before you start to work. We all know how that works out, don't we?

With that in mind, let me share a paradox with you:

Those who are sitting on their "blessed assurance", waiting 'til their ship comes in, waiting 'til they win the jackpot, waiting 'til they "hit the numbers", are going to die, spending all of eternity, doing, you guessed it, waiting 'til their ship comes in, or 'til hell itself freezes over, whichever comes first. Why, you ask? Because as long as they're waiting on someone else to make the first move, that's all that will happen: they will wait. And nothing will change. Have you ever drawn water from an old-fashioned well? If you have, then you know nothing comes up from the well unless you prime the pump first. You have to first take action before you can get the desired result. Get the picture?

So here's the other side of the coin:

It is only when you make a decision to move forward, to make changes, to re-write the script of your life, that you begin to receive the help you need, the help to carry out the vision that's in your heart, and ironically, the help that those sitting on the fence of indecision say they want, but won't take the proper steps to acquire. You don't have to have everything all figured out before you begin. You just have to begin.

It may be a corny, overused, even trite statement, but it is still true: You have to start where you are.

If the "disease" can be spelled D - O - U - B - T
Then here's how you spell the cure:

C - O - M - M - I - T - M - E - N - T

You must make a decision, then commit to act on that decision. Only then will the resources you need to carry out that decision come to the forefront. I believe it is best said by the prophet Habakkuk, who made this statement:

"And the Lord answered me and said, Write the vision, and engrave it plainly upon tablets that everyone who passes may [be able to] read [it easily and quickly] as he hastens by. For the vision is yet for an appointed time and it hastens to the end [fulfillment]; it will not deceive or disappoint. Though it tarry, wait [earnestly] for it, because it will surely come; it will not be behindhand on its appointed day."
- Habakkuk 2:2,3 (Amplified Bible)

You see, we make another big mistake, nearly as big as the first mistake, but just as devastating. I believe it is the main reason many people never get started. This is that mistake: we wrongly assume that any great endeavor we can accomplish must be achieved all by ourselves. We have this Lone Ranger, Lone Wolf, rugged individualist mentality that believes the old saying, "If you want something done right, you have to do it yourself," hook, line, and sinker. I believe we inherited this attitude from our school days. Remember? We were told me could study for tests, quizzes, and exams, in study groups, but how were we supposed to take those tests, quizzes, and exams? ALONE. Right? If we tried to collaborate and cooperate with our classmates we were accused of cheating, weren't we? In fact, what group of consumers flock most often to stores like Lowe's, Home Depot, Auto Zone, WalMart, Advance Auto Parts, NAPA, etc.? The same type of people we were trained to become from our youth: "DO IT YOURSELF"- ers...!!!!! Catching on???

Time for a reality check. Robert Kiyosaki, best-selling author of the Rich Dad educational series, explains that his mentor told him early in his business career:

"Business and investing are team sports." I submit to you that all success in any field of endeavor requires teamwork, but no teamwork can ever take place until someone makes the first move. It is strange but true, that you won't receive the help you need, the help the "fence-sitters" say they want, until you commit to taking the first step toward your goal. Like the above scripture says, once you make your vision, your objective, plain for all to see, people and resources from any and every direction will come to you in your time of need. Not all people, but the right people, will position themselves to help you fulfill your vision, your objective, your goal.

Think of the football team who has read the play (vision) which has been plainly laid out by their coach. At the beginning of the play, the quarterback hands the ball to the running back, who then runs toward the goal in front of him (representing fulfillment of the coach's vision). This running back is aided in his quest for the end zone (the appointed time of the coach's vision) by teammates on the offensive line, the receiving corps, and even the quarterback himself if needed, who block the obstacles in his path (the defenders assigned to stop him) and create open areas on the field of play through which the running back can advance down the field. The best illustration I can offer about the power of commitment can be found with this statement, which exemplifies its importance better than anything I have ever seen:

The Power of Commitment

"Until one is committed, there is hesitancy, the chance to draw back, always ineffectiveness. Concerning all acts of initiative (and creation) there is one elementary truth the ignorance of which kills countless ideas and splendid plans: that the moment one definitely commits oneself, then providence moves too. All sorts of things occur to help one that would never otherwise have occurred. A whole stream of events issues from the decision, raising in one's favour all manner of unforeseen incidents and meetings and material assistance, which no man could have dreamed would have come his way. Whatever you can do or dream you can, begin it. Boldness has genius, power and magic in it. Begin it now."
- Johann Wolfgang von Goethe (1749 - 1832)

So what shall we say to these things? Simply this: It doesn't matter whether you are on the top, in the middle, or at the bottom of the barrel. It doesn't matter who put you there, even if the "who" was you. And trying to figure out who is responsible for your current predicament in the barrel is a colossal waste of time. What is truly important is whether or not you decide you are going to get up and out of the barrel. Once you do that, and commit to making it happen, no devil in hell, or on the earth for that matter, will be able to keep you from reaching your goal. And don't forget, Providence Himself, The Great I AM, The Most High God is standing at the ready, with forces marshalled at His side, waiting for you to make your decision to get up out of that barrel. Once you do that, people and resources will come to your aid to help you keep the commitment you have made, so you will be able, at your appointed time, to fulfill the vision that He Himself has given you, for such a time as this.

Read it and reap...

Be blessed...

And we'll talk again...

15. Comparing Yourself With Others

Talk about practicing what you preach!

I recently wrote about not being bound up in enslavement to the guilt and shame of our past. I also talked about learning to let the past go in order to move on with one's life, and how important it is to forgive everyone you know who may have hurt you, but especially yourself.

How goes that saying, "Be careful what you wish for...", because you don't realize what you may be speaking into your life?

Well I just recently had the chance to reconnect with some friends I knew from over 20 years ago, which was a challenge for me, because unfortunately the last time I had contact with some of them we didn't part on the best of terms. There were a lot a hurt feelings, anger and bitterness to some degree. It took a long time for the hurt and anguish over the parting to subside. I will readily admit that my lack of maturity had a lot to do with what happened. I should have handled the situation better, but I didn't, and I had to deal with the consequences.

I guess looking back, I find myself dealing with what some would call "the pain of regret". But I believe that's only part of the story. The rest has to do with what has happened since that time, as I learned the other people I knew have gone on to "make something of themselves", having made significant achievements in life, and valuable contributions to society.

What I find myself struggling with are feelings of inferiority and inadequacy, because somehow I am tempted to fall into the trap of comparing myself with people I somehow believe to be superior to myself. It's all too easy to forget that despite any accolades we may or may not achieve, as mankind we are all in the same boat.

"For we dare not class ourselves or compare ourselves with those who commend themselves. But they, measuring themselves by themselves, and comparing themselves among themselves, are not wise." - II Corinthians 10:12

This scripture hit home with me a few years ago when I had the chance to attend a business conference.

One of the main speakers said something which spoke to the heart of the issue. She explained that when her children were young, she made it a point to teach them never to compare themselves to other people, because these comparisons would always be unfair. Not only unfair, but unfavorable, she explained, because when people make such comparisons they always compare their perceived weaknesses to what they believe to be other people's strengths. Never apples to apples. Never a level playing field.

I believe part of the reason so many people are depressed is because they try to fashion their lives after people they know, people they admire, even people they worship. Dr. Myles Munroe, best-selling author of "In Pursuit of Purpose," writes that "...too many people are born originals, yet they die copies." I like to sum this situation up with four simple words: SQUARE PEG, ROUND HOLE. So many people try to fashion their lives in ways that absolutely do not fit their personality. In his book "The Psychology of Winning", Dr. Denis Waitley refers to Losers as people who want to walk like, talk like, sound like, look like, somebody else. They measure themselves against standards set by others and deem themselves as failures when they don't make someone else's grade, or worse, because somebody told them they were failures.

Well, the way I see it, nobody on this earth qualifies as, according to Dr. Phil, "the repository of all truth and knowledge." At best, and often at worst, all we hold in most situations is an opinion. In somebody's opinion you look like a failure, but that somebody may not know your whole story. They only see a part of your life, but they don't see that part within the context of the entirety of your life story.

There's a popular gospel song from years ago whose main lyrics said, "Be patient with me; God is not through with me yet." Often we mistake a work in progress for a finished product, when we should look at each other with signs that read: UNDER CONSTRUCTION. Because we all are.

In closing, I'll share this with you. Anybody who knows me understands that I am a big-time sports fan. I tend to follow the major sports (baseball, football, hockey) along with soccer, golf and a few other minor ones. The most intriguing sport I have ever witnessed is the marathon.

Why the marathon? Because the unique aspect of the marathon is the fact that you can have more than one winner. You see, the marathon does not consider winners to be only the runners who finish first. The marathon recognizes those runners who FINISH. Period. When you run a marathon, as long as you finish, YOU WIN! No matter what obstacles, traps, pitfalls, setbacks you may encounter along the route to the end, as long as you cross the line, whether you're first or last, YOU WIN...!!! Nobody cares all that much about who finishes first. In fact, sometimes the ones who finish last are more celebrated than the one who breaks the tape.

So I would say, if you're still in the race, you still have a chance to win. So what if someone on the route is further up the road than you are? So what? The only "losers" are the ones who got off the road, or worse, never got on the road in the first place.

"Therefore we also, since we are surrounded by so great a cloud of witnesses, let us lay aside every weight (guilt, shame, fear, inferiority, condemnation, anguish, regret, etc.) and the sin which so easily ensnares us, and let us run with patient endurance the race that is set before us, looking unto Jesus, the author and finisher of our faith, who for the joy that was set before Him endured the cross, despising the shame, and has sat down at the right hand of the throne of God."
- Hebrews 12: 1,2

That pretty much sums it up. I believe I needed to share this as much as someone may have needed to read this. I don't mind "telling on myself" if it's going to help you get where you need to go. So get whatever you can from what I just shared, live fully, love often, forgive much (including yourself), and make someone's day...

You may not matter to the world,
But to someone in the world, you matter!

"A life is not important, except in the impact it has on other lives."
- Jackie Robinson (1919-1972)

Read it and reap...

Be blessed...

We'll talk again.....

16. The Key To Failure...

"I don't know the key to success, but I do know the key to failure: trying to please other people." - Bill Cosby

During the first week of July 2010, we as a nation celebrated our 234th birthday. We commemorated the day the Declaration of Independence stated the intentions of the original 13 colonies to establish themselves as a new nation upon the earth, an entity that never before existed. Every year on the 4th of July, we as Americans take time to pause and celebrate our way of life, our traditions, our culture, our heritage. In short, we celebrate our freedom.

Yet, as we remember the bravery and courage displayed by our Founding Fathers to establish freedom from British rule so many years ago, it is ironic that so many of the Founders' descendants in this country, namely us, do not appreciate, possess, or enjoy, the freedoms for which they pledged to one another their lives, their fortunes, and their sacred honor.

Long story short, Americans across the board are not free. When I say we are not free, I am not referring to what most people think about: economics, civil rights, discrimination, social injustice, unrest international and domestic, or anything of the sort. Nothing like that is what I'm talking about, but believe me when I tell you, we in America are in bondage. It is so subtle as to totally deceive even the most discerning "unum" among our "e pluribus", but it is destructive nonetheless.

What I am talking about is the slavery of opinion, approval and expectation that holds us in bondage. It is what Bill Cosby refers to when he says we become failures by trying in vain to please everyone at our own expense. Author Paul Coughlin ("No More Christian Nice Guy: When Being Nice, Instead of Good, Hurts Men, Women and Children") refers to it as the "disease to please". Author and speaker Joyce Meyer calls it "Approval Addiction" in her book of the same title. This theme is expressed in the popular saying, *"If Mama ain't happy, ain't nobody happy."*

Too many people, myself included, have fallen into the trap of measuring our success in life by the degree of happiness we bring to others. Don't get me wrong, there's nothing wrong with blessing others whenever the opportunity arises. What I'm talking about are the extreme cases (and there are more of them than we'd like to admit) where people consider themselves to be total failures if they are not living the type of life that is expected of them by others, most often by those people with whom they share their closest relationships: immediate family, relatives, friends, co-workers, siblings, parents, spouses. I think you get my drift.

As a result of this bondage, many people live in what Henry David Thoreau called "quiet desperation", wanting to press forward, to forge ahead with an exciting, exhilarating, challenging, stimulating, thrill-a-minute adventure, yet so many settle for a coach ticket when there's so much room up front in the first class section on the big 747 plane ride we call life.

WHY?????????

Why do we settle? Why do we compromise?? Why do we give up so easily??? Why do we throw in the towel when for so many of us, the fight hasn't really started? The opening bell hasn't even rung yet!!! And worst of all, WHY DO WE VOLUNTEER FOR THIS BONDAGE IN THE FIRST PLACE???????

Well I don't know about you, but this is the way I see it:

Starting in our childhood, I believe we have been sold a bill of goods. We were raised to believe some false notions.

First, I believe we were tricked into believing that to be a success in life meant that you could never experience any kind of failure, that failure was an absolute disaster, and that successful people win all the time, never experiencing any kind of setback, not even a minor or temporary one. Successful people were perfect, had no defects of any kind, never stumbled or tripped up (or over) anything, had "not a single hair out of place", etc. In other words, if you weren't perfect, you weren't successful, and if you weren't perfect or successful, something was wrong with you.

Failure meant punishment, shame, humiliation, and utter disgrace.

And second, which I believe is worst of all, was the delusion that you can't consider yourself a success unless you live up to everybody's expectations of you, no matter how unrealistic they are. We were somehow led to believe (I say "Mis"-led into believing) that we can't be happy with ourselves, cannot feel good about ourselves, unless everybody we know feels good about us. In the play "Death of a Salesman", main character Willy Loman tries in vain to explain his idea of success to his loved ones by saying that he always thought success meant "...being well liked". It seems as if we confuse success with popularity.

There is also the frustration that comes from dealing with people who mistakenly believe that your life is theirs to direct, that you somehow owe it to them to give your best efforts to make them happy, that their happiness is your responsibility. George Bernard Shaw wrote that these people insist that the world is obligated to making them happy. It's as if these people believe they know what is best for you.

And heaven forbid if you should have an original thought of your own. That would be a sacrilege.

Worst of all, we were taught as kids that in order to be successful you have to be good at everything under the sun. You couldn't afford to be weak in any area. In fact, we were told for as long as we can remember that if we wanted to be "well rounded individuals" (remember that one?) we had to work on our weaknesses, and let our strengths fall by the wayside. And if we were weak in any area we'd catch the "wrath of God" from parents, guardians, and whatever elders in our circle of family and friends that we knew, and that knew us. Why? Because we were supposed to be "perfect," that we were supposed to hold up the family honor, not make the family look bad, etc. So many of us today live with a weight of guilt, shame, fear, CONDEMNATION, because we somehow believe we are failures due to not living up to the expectations, unrealistic expectations, of our loved ones. And the sad part of that is this: the people we feel guilty about letting down, are also burdened by guilt about letting down the people, the elders, that placed expectations on them before we ever arrived on the scene.

It's a vicious cycle that seems to be a never-ending battle of frustration and despair.

But take heart, dear readers. Here is the reality:

While it is true that as children we are to be subject to those who came before us (you know, honor your father and mother, respect your elders, etc.), there is no reason why we should allow ourselves to be bound and burdened with a heavy load of condemnation, despair and hopelessness. That is not how things are supposed to be.

In I Corinthians 13:11, the Apostle Paul writes this eye-opening statement:

"When I was a child, I spoke as a child, I understood as a child, I thought as a child; but when I became a man (WHEN I GREW UP), I put away childish things."

Did you catch that? What he said, in a nutshell, is this: there is a time and place for us to be obedient to our elders in all things, even as it relates to reaching for high standards they may set for you. But once you grow up, once you reach the place where you are responsible for making your own decisions, the time for those type of boundaries comes to and end. Like the panicked Marine said in the movie Aliens, "GAME OVER, MAN!!!"

Yet we have so many grown ups saddled with feelings of guilt, failure, inferiority over things that happened in their past, 30, 40, 50, 60 or more years ago. Sometimes it's as little as 5, 10, 15 years ago, but you get the point. They don't realize that the word "fail" is a verb, not a noun. Failure is an event, not a person. In this day and age, when mistakes are made (and EVERYBODY MAKES MISTAKES) corrections can be made. You see, we have a great example of how to make corrections, and it's very simple. Last I checked, we still have and use pencils in our everyday lives. And on the end of virtually every pencil, there is a "high tech" correction device called an eraser. You can choose to correct your mistakes if you want. You don't have to suffer throughout your entire existence over mistakes you made in the past. You can correct them and move on. One of the best ways to correct a past mistake is to forgive. Yes, forgive. You may think this is foolish, but hear me out. The mistake I'm talking about is not the transgressive act itself, it's the grudge we often find ourselves holding onto as a result of that action.

And you may think I'm only talking about forgiving others for what they did to you. Guess again, Sparky. I'm also talking about, I'm ESPECIALLY talking about, forgiving the one Michael Jackson sung about, "The Man in the Mirror". I'm talking about YOU. You need to forgive yourself for failing to live up to unrealistic expectations, because nobody is able to hold up a false standard. And then get around to forgiving those who unknowingly (or even knowingly) wronged you, because it's most likely they didn't realize what they were doing, anyway.

You see, you have a choice. You can choose to allow the past, good or bad, to haunt you, or you can choose not to. It's all up to you. You can choose to hold on to those false expectations to determine whether or not you are a success, or you can choose to let them go. It's all up to you. You can choose to live the rest of your life with the weight of others' opinions, and expectations, hoping in vain to gain their approval, or you can choose not to. It's up to you. You can choose (or not choose) to realize that you are only responsible for living one life on this earth, and for making the most of that life. That one life belongs to you, and no one else.

Oh, by the way, here's another reality check for you: everybody you know is not going to agree with you, no matter what you say or do, good or bad. And you'll never stop people from talking about you, no matter what you say or do. When you think about it, there are three times when people talk about you: the day you're born, the day you die, AND EVERY DAY IN BETWEEN. So don't think you can gain people's approval by doing with your life what you think they would expect you to do. You can't gain their approval on those terms, and you never will.

So make a conscious choice to live your life in the way that brings you the most peace and joy. And you'll be able to say like the writer of Psalm 118.24: *"This is the day that the Lord has made; I WILL(INGLY CHOOSE TO) rejoice and be glad in it."*

Read it and reap....

Be blessed!!!

We'll talk again soon....

17. The Hardest Thing To Do

Sometimes the hardest thing to do is to start again after experiencing a setback. You're embarrassed, humiliated, ashamed. You want to stay in bed and pull the covers over your head. You doubt your abilities, your convictions. You doubt your dreams, your goals, your desires, calling them silly, wishful thinking, unrealistic. You try to convince yourself that what you want is foolish, that you should be "real," get a life, etc.

Well in that moment of frustration, that moment of disappointment and despair is THE EXACT MOMENT when you should try again. Give your dreams another shot. Because it is during that down time that you come to realize that in order to accomplish your dreams, goals, and desires, you cannot do it alone. Your ultimate success is going to be a team effort, with people and with resources coming alongside to help you when you need it most. The reason you need that setback, strangely enough, is because you need a dose of humility in order to learn how to win with grace. It is said that after many defeats resulting from unsuccessful bids for elected office, Abraham Lincoln won election to public office only once:

when he was elected 16th President of the United States. One of President Lincoln's best recognized character traits was his humility. I believe this quality was forged by many setbacks he suffered, politically (and personally), setbacks which prepared him to guide this nation through the four turbulent years we know today as the Civil War. At war's end, Lincoln's humility was on full display, as he sought to make provision for his vanquished enemy, even as he accepted the terms of their surrender.

In the desert Moses was found tending his father-in-law's flocks, having been humbled by shame from a murder he committed decades earlier. God sought him out for a special assignment, knowing full well that Moses had been humbled by his previous experience.

If you are reading this and wondering how this could apply to you, ask yourself if you've ever experienced a setback in life that left you hurt, embarrassed, humiliated, ashamed, and feeling like you can never show your face in public again. I cannot tell for certain, since I don't know you, but I believe you have experienced such a setback at one point in your life, maybe more.

If that is you, listen very closely: I believe the pain of that moment may, through humility, have positioned you to experience a triumph that will so far outweigh your setback, it may seem to you that the setback, failure, defeat, whatever you call it, may have happened to someone else, but not you. Sometimes that humiliation is necessary, because it is only in a time of humility that you can learn how to win with grace. As Willie Jolley's best-selling book proclaims:

"A Setback Is a Setup For a Comeback"
(www.williejolley.com)

Read it and reap...

Be blessed...

And we'll talk again...

"Courage doesn't always roar. Sometimes courage is the little voice at the end of the day that says I'll try again tomorrow."
- Mary Anne Radmacher

18. A Friend Loves At All Times

"A friend loves at all times, and is born, as is a brother, for adversity." - Proverbs 17:17

Friend: a person attached to another by feelings of affection or personal regard

A friend loves you in every situation, any event, any circumstance. They may not always like what you do, they may not always agree with you, they may not see eye to eye with you in all things, but they like who you are. That's the important thing. They are interested in who you are, not in what you do, and they do not think they would like you better if you would just change. They like you for who you are, right now. At this very moment.

Such friendship is extremely rare these days, and I think I know why. Almost from the time we are born we get hints (some subtle, others not so much) that the only way we can get ahead in life, that we can be successful, is to make sure the "right" people like us (whomever they may be; I have yet to meet a "right" person myself), and to make sure we do everything within our power to curry their favor.

We do not cultivate relationships for mutual benefit, but for personal gain, even if doing so means we have to pretend to be someone we're not. So in effect, we are taught to tell "little white lies," to be dishonest, to deny our true selves. Some attempt to justify the practice, calling it "protocol." I call it pretense, phoniness, hypocrisy. I don't want to see your mask; I want to see you. If I am to make the proper assessment of who you are, I need to know who you are. And I need you to know who I am. That's the only way I can be your friend, and you can be mine.

It may be hard to believe, but when you have a true friend, you will find that they do not have any lofty expectations of you, realistic or unrealistic. All a friend wants from you is for you to share with them the following: mutual respect, affection, and personal regard. And the best part is, you do not have to be perfect. A true friend will love you on only one condition: F.A.A. (Flaws And All) What a contrast that is with what we try to pass off as relationships these days. Marriages today are especially on shaky ground, because husbands and wives have forgotten what it means to be each other's friend. We've scrapped notions of affection, personal regard, and mutual respect.

We've thrown away the friendship aspect of matrimony and replaced it with conditions: I'll be your friend if you impress me, I'll be your lover if you please me. Gimme, Gimme, Gimme. We pledge unconditional love to one another, but let our beloved slip up once too often, and without warning we call off the deal. We stop being friends and lovers, and slowly morph into each other's judge, jury and executioner. As a result husbands and wives find themselves walking on eggshells around one another, becoming emotionally distant in the process, trying their best to keep a fragile peace that is nonexistent, straining to avoid tripping on marital landmines scattered all over the rugged terrain of their relationship. Such distance, when continued over time, takes husbands and wives down a road that neither of them intended to travel. Do I really need to tell you where that road leads? I didn't think so.

If any of this seems farfetched to you, let me ask you a question: Do you know for a certainty that you have friends that you love and love you in return just for being who you are? Or do the people you know act as judge and jury toward you, in an effort to get you to tie yourself in knots for the purpose of impressing them before they even consider "liking" you? Letting you into their circle? Their clique? Their group? Their posse? Think about it...

Here's a suggestion: if you're not sure you have any friends, or even if you're not sure how to make friends, I propose the following:

"A man who has friends must himself be friendly..." - Proverbs 18:24

There are no two ways around it: in order to have friends at some point in time you need to make the first move, to show people that you are a friendly individual, and take the risk that they'll return your show of friendship and good will. If they choose not to, don't take it personally. Remember that was their choice, not yours. You didn't make them reject you in that instance. They chose to do so. The best thing to do in that case is keep it movin'. It's their loss, not yours, as they missed out on getting the chance to know someone as special as you.

As for me, I will cherish the friends I have, whether I have made new ones, or had the opportunity to rekindle some friendships from days gone by. I refuse to make a priority of those people who saw me as nothing more than an option in their lives; I refuse to look back on those moments of loss. Instead, I will treasure these special "family" members who have allowed me into their lives, knowing that they are those special people who make living on earth all the more worthwhile, no matter what I face. I look forward to visiting them, online or in person, and I dread having to part. They mean that much to me.

So let me sum up the importance of friendship in life with the following:

"Don't walk in front of me, I may not follow.
Don't walk behind me, I may not lead.
Just walk beside me and be my friend."
- Albert Camus

"Who finds a faithful friend, finds a treasure."
- Jewish saying

"A true friend is someone who thinks you are a good egg even though (s)he knows that you are slightly cracked." - Bernard Meltzer

Read it and reap...

Be blessed...

And we'll talk again...

19. I Didn't Come This Far....!!!

In the Disney movie "Finding Nemo," we follow the story of Marlin, a clownfish in a desperate search to find his kidnapped son, Nemo. Along the way he makes new friends who guide him in his search, but something even more important takes place. Marlin finds himself having to overcome challenges, rising to the occasion time and time again, in ways he never before would have imagined. It is a classic example of someone leaving their comfort zone, overcoming fears, doubts, insecurities, even regrets, on the way to achieving his desired objective, the rescue of his son.

By the time his quest is completed, he has gained something even more important and ultimately gratifying than just the ability to conquer himself, or his obstacles. He wins the love and respect of his son, who sees him not just as his dad, but as his hero.

On the way to rescuing Nemo, Marlin has one transcendent, transforming, signature moment which defines the change in his character as a result of his quest.

Just as he arrives at his destination to find his son, he and a traveling buddy (Dory) are swallowed by a pelican, who believes his morning meal is complete with Marlin and Dory's capture. Well Marlin didn't get that memo. Just as he's on the way to being digested, Marlin spreads his fins to lodge himself in the pelican's throat, then in a fit of anger (what I like to call his "had it up to here" moment) he shouts at the top of his gills:

I DIDN'T COME THIS FAR TO BE BREAKFAST!!!!!

It was at that moment, after having conquered this latest of many obstacles, challenges, adversities he had to face, Marlin knew he would not be denied, no matter what other difficulties may be thrown at him. Remembering that single moment from the movie inspired me to write this, because there are readers who right now are in the same situation where Marlin found himself. You know who you are. You have dealt with all kinds of trouble, setbacks, problems, challenges, adversity. It seems like everyone and everything that could come against you has done so, from all directions, seemingly at once.

Yet in spite of all these obstacles you are still able to make significant progress toward attaining your objectives. You have experienced valuable growth in the process as well.

Then just when you're on the brink of seeing that finish line you have looked forward to crossing for what seems like an eternity, just when the victory, the success you have longed for can not only be felt on your fingertips, you can practically taste it on the tip of your tongue...Some challenge, some obstacle, some adversity comes out of nowhere that threatens to pull everything apart at the seams which you have worked so hard to put together, cause a complete breakdown, and undo all the good you have accomplished in reaching this point, when you are literally on the verge of achieving for yourself a major victory.

At this point you probably expect me to ask you if you're going to get "angry" or not, or question whether or not you should. Dear reader, I have too much respect for you and your intelligence to insult you like that. I'm not going to sugar coat the situation, either. Let's be real here. OF COURSE YOU'RE GOING TO GET MAD!!! That's not the issue, and it never has been the issue.

If you didn't get mad I'd be shocked. You will be mad, upset, furious, ready to spit fire, all of the above. Whenever someone, or something comes along to detour or derail you, it is normal, even expected that you won't like it. Don't be phony, be real. Stop trying to play it off, you are not Cool Hand Luke. You get mad. It happens. Deal with it.

Here's the real question you need to answer:

HOW will you get mad?

Don't go "out to lunch" on me. This is vital. How you respond when you're hoppin' mad about a last minute detour is critical when it comes to reaching your goals. Let me explain. There are two ways to respond to a last second complication that threatens your success. One way is the popular, "make nice," "woe is me, sym-pa-thee, just for me" version that causes one to sit down, suck his thumb, boo hoo hoo, and whine about how "it's just not fair" that every time they're about to do something good, something comes along that ruins everything. This is the one "Party Animal" you want to avoid like the plague: The Pity Party Animal.

Don't let this person's fatal, pessimistic view of life infect you. They are highly contagious.

On the other hand, you could be like Marlin who almost strangled a pelican from the inside out, knowing he'd have to do so if it meant he had no other choice in order to save his son. Just like he yelled out, almost in a primal scream, you too may find yourself yelling to no one in particular (it's not as crazy as some would like you to believe), something that sounds like this:

I DIDN'T COME THIS FAR TO QUIT! I DIDN'T COME THIS FAR TO LOSE!

I DIDN'T COME THIS FAR TO GIVE UP!

I DIDN'T COME THIS FAR TO THROW IT ALL AWAY!

I DIDN'T COME THIS FAR, AND I DIDN'T GET THIS CLOSE,
TO HAVE YOU TAKE MY VICTORY AWAY FROM ME!

AND IF YOU THINK I'M GOING TO JUST STAND HERE AND LET YOU WALK OFF WITH MY SWEET TRIUMPH AFTER ALL I WENT THROUGH TO GET IT, THEN THINK AGAIN, BECAUSE I'M NOT THE ONE!!!

There are other examples, but I believe you get the picture. You have to be mad enough to stand up to your challenge and declare that if only one of you is going to be left standing when the dust settles, either you or your challenge, you know it's going to be you in the end.

This last obstacle is a final test to see how badly you want to reach your goal, and how much you are willing to do whatever it takes to clear that last hurdle. It doesn't matter if it's the biggest obstacle you face, or the baddest. What matters is that it is there, and it is real. How you handle it, even though you're mad, will go a long way toward determining how soon you reach the summit and conquer your mountain, or if you do so at all.

So go ahead. Get mad. But when you do, don't pull back. Don't lose heart. Don't give up. Don't give in. Give your all. Move ahead. Go forward. And remember,

YOU DIDN'T COME THIS FAR TO BE DEFEATED, YOU CAME THIS FAR TO WIN!!!

And once you do win, once you do taste sweet victory and glorious triumph, you will be able to say:

"I have fought a good fight. I have kept the faith. I have finished my course." - II Timothy 4:7

Read it and reap...

Be blessed everybody...

And we'll talk again...

20. You've Saved The Best For Last

"For our light, momentary affliction (this slight distress of the passing hour) is ever more and more abundantly preparing and producing and achieving for us an everlasting weight of glory [beyond all measure, excessively surpassing all comparisons and all calculations, a vast and transcendent glory and blessedness never to cease!]"
- II Corinthians 4:17 Amplified Bible

Maybe you feel left out. You're standing on the side of the road, watching the parade of life march by. Maybe you feel obsolete, as if your skills and talents are no longer valid, no longer useful, no longer valuable. Maybe you see the next generation doing things you longed to do at an earlier time in your life. But for whatever reason, fear, doubt, negative opinion, lack of confidence, whatever, you didn't take action toward those goals. Or maybe you're just in a rut, going through the motions, doing the same thing day after day after day, hoping for things to change. Your life has become so routine you could hire someone to stand in for you and not a soul would know the difference.

If what you've just read in any way describes you, then I have some good news for you. You are the product of two lives: the life you have lived, and the life you have yet to experience. The really good news is that your life isn't over, it's really just getting started. You're just getting warmed up. Your future can still be infinitely more exciting, more thrilling, more challenging than your past. Even if your past was exciting, thrilling, and challenging already, your future can be better still. You see, all of us were designed for growth. From cradle to grave, there is always something new to learn, new to encounter, new to achieve, new to conquer. You haven't mastered yet all the challenges in life you are to face. Heck, you haven't even met them all yet. And what's more, you have no idea how quickly your life can change for the better, no matter how dire your situation seems to be right now.

Even if you think you've failed, that you don't measure up, can't compare, that you do not deserve anything good in your life, there is still a chance for you to turn things around. You may think you can't win, you can't make it, that you'll never win. Don't cash in your chips just yet. You are much too valuable for that.

Again I say, you are a product of two lives: the life you have lived, and the life you have yet to live. Separate by-products come from your two lives. The first by-product is called MEMORIES. These are your recollections of the experiences you have had up to this point, the good, the not so good, and everything in between. They have molded and shaped you into the person you have become. The second by-product, though not as established as the first, is the more important of the two. This one is called LESSONS. These make up the sum total of the wisdom you have gained through the years, whether from pain or from pleasure. This category is important for two reasons. First, newfound wisdom puts you in position to gain deeper meaning from all your experiences, whether past, present or future. And second, which is even more important, you have the opportunity to share the lessons you have learned, the wisdom you have gained, with those of the next generation, the up and comers who need to benefit of what life has taught you, in much the same way you learned at the feet of the elders who went before you.

Now it is your turn to take up the mantle of authority and leadership that has been passed down to you, so you can be a conduit of learning, a wellspring of wisdom and knowledge for those who have yet to follow the trail which you have blazed.

Such training for the next generation cannot be underestimated in its importance, because no matter how much technology changes, with advancements seemingly developing at light speed everywhere you turn, true wisdom is as priceless as it is timeless. No gadget can hold a candle to the wisdom of the ages, regardless of how shiny its bells and whistles may be.

And best of all no matter how much knowledge may increase on the earth in the coming days there is no substitute for wisdom and maturity. These qualities never go out of style. No new gadget or "widget" can rob you of the inheritance and the legacy that is rightfully yours. So chin up and cheer up. If your life hasn't yet been what you'd like it to be, you still have time to live in such a way that your future can be better than you ever imagined, so far surpassing your past that you may forget what manner of difficulty you once endured. So bright you need to wear shades.

Take heart. You have saved your best for last, and for you the best is yet to come.

"The glory is this latter temple shall be greater than the former, says the Lord of hosts. And in this place I will give peace, says the Lord of hosts. - Haggai 2:9

Read it and reap...

Be blessed...

And we'll talk again...

Invitation

Hello again. Thank you for taking your time to read my book. If you'd like a chance to learn more about what you've read, as well as take the chance to share any wisdom you have gained from the special people in your life, I invite you to visit the Pearls group page on Facebook.

It is a community where all the members share wisdom and grow together in understanding. Please feel free to visit any time, and invite your friends to do the same.

I hope you enjoyed this book, and that I have shared something with you which you can use to win the battles you face in your daily life.

Be blessed, today and every day....

Earl

www.ingramcontent.com/pod-product-compliance
Ingram Content Group UK Ltd.
Pitfield, Milton Keynes, MK11 3LW, UK
UKHW041941190726
13854UKWH00004B/1717